THE AMERICAN SERFS

The
American Serfs

by PAUL GOOD

G. P. Putnam's Sons

NEW YORK

Copyright © 1968 by Paul Good

Library of Congress Catalog
Card Number: 68-8320

PRINTED IN THE UNITED STATES OF AMERICA

For Martin Luther King, Jr., who was killed on the eve of his ultimate campaign to end the American serfdom

The author wishes to thank the following for permission to quote excerpts from their works:

"The Negro in American Agriculture" by Calvin L. Beale, from *The American Negro Reference Book*, John P. Davis (ed.), reprinted by permission of Prentice-Hall, Inc. Copyright © 1966 by Prentice-Hall, Inc., Englewood Cliffs, New Jersey.

The Mind of the South by Wilbur J. Cash, reprinted by permission of Alfred A. Knopf, Inc. Copyright © 1941 by Alfred A. Knopf, Inc., New York, New York.

Contents

9

"Although the economic well-being and prosperity of the United States have progressed to a level surpassing any achieved in world history and although these benefits are widely shared throughout the Nation, poverty continues to be the lot of a substantial number of our people. ...It is therefore the policy of the United States to eliminate the paradox of poverty in the midst of plenty in this Nation...."

—Economic Opportunity Act of 1964

"To fail to understand the causes of ghetto frustration and violence and to refuse to recognize and attack the underlying forces is to perpetuate more frustration and more violence. Such a course threatens the very foundation of our Republic. We in rural America have a responsibility to help alleviate the pressures that we have imposed on our cities."

—Secretary of Agriculture Orville Freeman

"Rural poverty is so widespread, and so acute, as to be a national disgrace, and its consequences have swept into our cities violently.... Most of the rural South is one vast poverty area."

—President's National Advisory Commission on Rural Poverty

"They call this a war on poverty. But what kind of a war is this when most people don't really want you to win?"

—OEO Florida Migrant Director William Johnson

"Not for you to have nothin', that's what they really want."

—Buck Sims, evicted Alabama Negro farmer

11

THE AMERICAN SERFS

1

The Graveyard
on Dick Silver Hill

THE graveyard lies in a thicket by a field plowed now for soybeans and dust-dry under the Alabama sun. It is one of the last fields Buck Sims ever planted in cotton. He had heard that they had plowed up the graves but found this was not true. The stones were untouched, some time-tumbled and hard to find in a profusion of grass and brush in the cool shadows from water oak, sweet gum, and pine. He knelt and pulled back a thorny bush from a granite marker sunk comfortably into the earth where it had been placed 142 years ago. The shallow outline of a dove was visible above the inscription:

Joseph Sims
Born 1825

"Now he was the uncle of my great-granddaddy Peter Sims," Buck Sims said. "His grave is over yonder. What's that date say? An' watch your hand for snakes. They're thick as fleas aroun' here. 'Peter Sims, born 1837, died 1912.' I don't remember him but he was the daddy of my granddaddy Dave Sims. Granddaddy told me all the stories about this place. There's a cousin of his someplace, Hampton Sims. He fought in the Civil War for the South an' died somewhere about 1920 at ninety years of age."

All the headstones were there, cold as death to the touch

despite the heat of the July afternoon. But the symbols of death were not repellent on Dick Silver Hill. They seemed fitting instead of fearful; stone and earth, life and death in natural communion over long years of bright days and quiet nights. Generations who had lived on the land, first as slaves and then as freedmen, had been returned to it in a clan in a tranquil place, so that there was not the sense of life broken but of an eternal living circle completed.

"The reason they call this place Dick Silver Hill," Sims said, "was explained to me by my granddaddy. There was a slave by that name an' when he felt like they was doin' him wrong he'd run off to a den he'd dug in the side of the hill over yonder there where it slopes down into the swamp. I used to look as a boy but it was probly fell in an' I never could find it. Anyway, he had it closed up so tight they couldn't discover it to get at him an' fetch him back. When things quieted down, he'd come back out. My granddaddy knew Dick Silver as a old man an' he said Silver'd tell how they used to whip him an' he'd say, 'Don't never let nobody whip you.' My granddaddy, he was a tough man an' he taught his boys to be tough."

To be tough was to endure but not to prosper. Buck Sims' father was a tenant farmer on the same land the family had worked back to Indian times in western Alabama. But when he died in 1930, Buck, who was twelve, and brothers a few years on either side of him had to quit school to help their mother, plowing and planting ten acres of cotton. A man's work.

By that time the family had been farming the same portion of white man's land for well over a century as slaves, sharecroppers, and tenants. However, the headstones on the hill in the summer of 1967 told a descendant tale of the family's fortunes. The last grave with a proper marker (dates chiseled, dove winging) belonged to Buck Sims' father. But his mother's grave was marked only by a length of bare lead pipe, hammered into the ground like a vampire's stake in a horror movie. Sims stood beside it, a slight man with graying hair and moustache, his tone of voice apologizing for his failure to provide as a free man what his forbears had been able to provide as slaves.

"She died in 1952," he said. "There wasn't no money to get a stone, everything was tight then, so—I did what I could to mark it with that pipe. She deserves better. She held us all together. An' there's my daughter, now she don't have nothin' at all an' she should. But I can't make it no way. You see, tenant farmin' hereabouts has been down, down, down. Take '64. With nine acres. . . ."

His daughter died a year ago a month after childbirth, leaving her parents the infant and another daughter to raise. There is only a mound of earth flattening out and a rusted tin can holding the dry stalks of dead flowers to mark where she is buried. Her father moved to it, explaining, talking about tenant farming in the present tense, although it was past for him. Because Sims would never again raise another crop on that land farmed by his family since before Alabama became a state.

He had been evicted.

His house had been knocked down, burned up.

His daughter had given birth in a tent that was the family's only shelter after eviction during an Alabama winter, which is not gentle. Unable to afford a hospital, she had lain with her new baby for weeks until she died in that cold tent.

So Buck Sims, along with thousands of other black Southern farmers who had existed on the land at the pleasure of white men, had become part of an impoverished and rootless Southern peasantry, medieval serfs in the most modern nation on the earth. But without even the serf's scrap of land to live and die on.

As he stood there, discoursing on bales to the acre, the price of a bale, a jetliner made a slow beeline in the top of the sky, reality and symbol of an age infinitely remote from him and the hill where his dead are buried. The dead might still tenant the earth, but the living were dispossessed, and Buck Sims, great-grandson of a slave, is a living wraith who will never rest on Dick Silver Hill.

2

Figures in Black and White

BUCK SIMS is neither average nor unique. He is not a Southern Everyman but a poor, black Southern man, still in his productive years and condemned to unproductive poverty by a combination of inept and inhuman forces operating in the North and the South, inside the government and out, and through all of us. The fact that he is Negro accounts for *his* present state. But there are also white Southern men whose families, like Sims', hunger for hope, partake of poverty. In an age of hyperbole, words like "poverty," along with others like "love," lose their essence except to those who experience them. Those most knowledgeable are often mute; there are things too deep and complicated to explain.

But today explanations are in order. The South used to be a drawling world away, a repository of myths about happy darkies and hospitable whites dwelling in pastoral coexistence. No more. The myth is dead, murdered along with black men who tried to change a racist system. And the South is no longer remote. It has been brought north and west by Negroes fleeing what they could not alter, an incredible migration of three million people in the last twenty-five years. They come bearing burdens of bitterness, physical and mental scars suffered under semibondage, and long memories of racial humiliations. The North has not been kind. In its cramped ghettos black has honed his hatred of white against the memory of Southern persecution and the disillusion of Northern betrayal. Murderous emotions are let loose in riot that verges toward rebellion. And each day the sullen ghetto swells a little more with new migrants who have decided that nothing can be as bad as staying south. There is pathos and danger in this headlong flight whipped on by poverty, abetted by federal inertia, and encouraged by Southern white efforts to humble, to thwart, and ultimately to squeeze black men from the Southland. There is also an opportunity—fast disappearing—to create a Southern environment that draws men to it as strongly as the present misery repels them.

In 1967, circumstances called attention to poor conditions in Mississippi, and the country at large was made aware that in this Croesus of a nation black children went to bed hungry and woke up sick to live or die as best they could.[1] The country had been unaware. It could sight a landing space on the moon, but it could not see a shack in the Delta. It could bounce TV shows off a satellite, but it could not hear a man on earth plead for work. It could spend $800 million a year on food and clothing for its dogs and cats while children cried for milk and shoes.

Pollsters report a majority of the American population worried about being overweight. But the underweight, the hunger of fellow citizens, was not a cause for national concern. It is true that once poverty in Mississippi was "discovered," a predictable outcry against it arose in Washington and elsewhere.[2] The outcry was neither as anguished nor enduring as might have been expected from a civilized people learning of its brothers in despair. Still, it was a sign that an atrophied conscience was not dead. But in the concern over Mississippi there was a tendency to isolate its poverty as a cruel product of that state's peculiar racist obsession *when truly it was only the most gross example of rural poverty endemic to the South.*[3]

The truth is that in all the shallow publicity about the old order changing in the South by virtue of new federal law, the essential unchanging disorder in lives made chaotic by poverty continues unabated. Look at any economic distribution map of the United States. Dots signify the deprived. A peppering of need in the Southwest becomes dense as it merges into the Black Belt in Arkansas and Mississippi, then spreads like a blot on the map east through Alabama and Georgia, and north through the Carolinas, Tennessee, and Kentucky.

This book attempts to tell some of the story of that Southern poverty, its causes and consequences, and possible remedies. It is intended to tell the story primarily through the lives of those living it, although statistics are inevitably involved. And there are ample statistics, forests of figures which, in their density, by their proliferating growth, suggest that compilation signifies progress and that we are getting somewhere. When the only place we really have got is deeper into the forest.

The figures come from government agencies skilled at counting what they do not alter, and from concerned private groups and dedicated individuals deploring what they cannot change. Their impressive sweep takes in millions of lives, decades of time, and they provide necessary perspectives in the total picture of a country with a Gross National Product of $800 billion a year. We see that the picture is badly out of balance in its southern quadrant, where a fourth of the forty million whites (eleven million people) live below poverty levels along with two-thirds of eleven million Negroes (seven million people).

What we do with those statistics determines their usefulness and our own humanity; set down in black and white, they will not go away; nor will the questions arising from the lives of the ciphers so thoroughly numbered. So many poor have no federal food programs available to them; [4] how does one mother feel giving her baby a bottle of sugar water instead of milk? So many poor children—black and white—drop out of high school; [5] how does one child cope with the humiliation of going to class in cast-off clothes and indulging in the luxury of homework when the family doesn't need a scholar but a provider? So many unemployed fathers cannot even read these words that relate directly to their plight.[6]

Figures are valuable. Figures do not (except now and then) lie. Without them, individual tales of privation in this report might be dismissed as invention or surmise. And still might be, even in the face of some more facts and figures that will not go away:

Dr. Vivian Henderson, reporting for the Southern Regional Council in *The Economic Status of Negroes in the Nation and in the South,* found that overall personal per capita income in the South quadrupled since 1940, while still remaining 75 percent of the national average. Southern Negro families had half the income of whites in the South, while individual Negroes earned only two-fifths as much as their white counterparts.

The U.S. Civil Rights Commission 1965 report "Equal Opportunity in Farm Programs" showed that the 1959 median income of rural Southern Negro *families* living off the farm was $1,529 (about $30 a week, well under poverty level and since worsened) while comparable white families earned $3,504 (a shade above poverty).

Approaching it another way, a formula devised by Miss Mollie Orshansky of the Social Security Administration produces 1964 figures for the Deep South states showing 75 percent of Negroes on farms and 69 percent of Negroes off farms in rural areas were poverty-stricken. The white poor percentages were 26 and 19 respectively.

The Bureau of Census reported in 1960 that about 70 percent of rural Negro homes and 27 percent of white were deteriorating and dilapidated. But no government agency went into these shacks to inquire how families were eating, if children were hungry, if bodies were immediately sick from malnutrition or hunger's long-range effect on bone, nerve, and muscle. How can such an oversight be explained in a nation that casts itself in the role of demographic godfather to half the world? The role's validity becomes suspect abroad when the problem continues unsolved at home, where it does not require exotic alien knowledge to know that if you sow the statistics of poverty you must reap hunger, ignorance, and stunted lives. And sometimes, nothing comes up at all.

Indifference to need has grown to a national habit. Southern officialdom generally treats victims of poverty as if they had committed some crime, thereby losing their civil and human rights. This permits disengagement from the poor by officialdom, or at best grudging doles, while leaving the official Christian conscience clear. Deep South states are still struggling to get into the American economic mainstream and some have a long way to go. In order to help, they need help. Sometimes it is there. The federal government annually offers millions in welfare monies that are not accepted. Is it because the money is tainted, coming from the reviled seat of central authority? No. It's a matter of priority. Highway funds from the same source are snatched up before ink has dried on the appropriation bill. But in 1967, thirteen Southern and border states forfeited more than a quarter of a *billion* federal welfare dollars because they would not put up supplemental funds to raise their per capita welfare payments to the national average of $31.61 a month.[7] These supplemental funds are less than one-third the federal contribution.

What does this forfeiture mean to the needy individual? In Mississippi, for example, it means that a dependent child is given $9.30 *a month* for his food, clothes, books, and recreation. That payment is composed of $7.75 in federal money, $1.55 in state. If Mississippi would contribute a total of $7.90 a month to that child, Washington would give $24.10 to bring it up to the average, an average which in itself is a crumb thrown from the groaning national table. Mississippi will not do even this. The federal government exerts almost no control over how the pittance Mississippi does accept is doled out, and Mississippi welfare law, in common with that of her sister states, is merely Draconian.[8] If Washington had the same indifferent attitude toward monies it heaps on the state National Guards, the Guardsmen would soon be drilling with broomsticks. They aren't. Again, it is a question of priorities, this time national ones.

While a specious poor-mouth defense may be made for niggardly welfare payments, no such defense is possible on the reluctance or refusal to participate in federal food programs. The Department of Agriculture presents its 1967 figures for the South showing that only two million of eight million certified poor are receiving these programs. This year, nearly 900 of the 3,090 counties in America had no federal food programs, although virtually every county in the country has poor people who need help to eat.

From the states' fiscal standpoint, the most painless program is surplus commodities. A county qualifies by establishing that enough poor people there (50 percent of the population) need food. The federal government, at its expense, ships in surplus products purchased by the Department of Agriculture, with each monthly portion containing about $5 worth of food. The cost to counties in distribution is a few cents per person, but Washington assumes this in appropriate cases.

The alternative is food stamps. Provided by the federal government, these enable the poor to purchase coupons redeemable in food stores in excess of face value. The Agriculture Department reluctantly cut stamp prices last year in the face of disclosures from private groups like the Citizens Crusade Against Poverty that stamps were priced beyond the reach of many needing them. Currently, the lowest stamp purchase price for a single person with an income of nothing to $30 a month is 50 cents for $12 worth of stamps. But the authorized cuts are still not in effect in many counties where local authority—unchecked by Washington—sets its own standards to suit its own theories on how the poor should be managed. A county may have either commodities or food stamps. A trend has developed in counties accepting commodities to switch over to stamps. The reasons are many, including pressure from grocers and food chains, to whom free food for the hungry is anathema. Experience has shown that when a country goes from commodities to stamps, participation drops at least 50 percent. What happens to the 50 percent who disappear from the roles is anybody's guess.

Grim revelations out of Mississippi shook loose these truths from government statistical cupboards and in the process demonstrated the obvious—that Southern black poverty is infinitely more desperate than its white counterpart. Dr. Albert Britton, Jr., a Negro physician of Jackson, Mississippi, made a brilliant and bone-chilling exposition of the racial facts of life and death in his state.[9] He told a Senate subcommittee that the death rate for black infants between one month and one year was five times that of white. The overall infant mortality rate was 53.1 per thousand compared with a white Mississippi rate of 23.1, almost the exact national percentage. Dr. Britton catalogued black Mississippians' deprivations from womb to grave. Often it is a journey of only a few hours, sometimes an arduous lifetime. But long or short, it is the black man's lot throughout the Deep South. And the poor man's lot throughout America. Dr.

H. Jack Geiger of Tufts-New England Medical Center says the health of the nation's poor is "an ongoing national disaster." He estimates that poor Americans are four times as likely to die before age thirty-five as the average citizen. Dr. Geiger reports that nonwhite infant mortality in 1940 was 70 percent higher than white. By 1962, it had increased to 90 percent. To be poor is deadly. To be black and poor is to be doomed.

Dr. Henderson's report sums up the Southern Negro's losing battle to raise income to white levels with the heading "Income —Negroes Running Fast to Stand Still." [10] The U.S. Civil Rights Commission Report previously cited says: "Every 10 years the census has reported a widening gap in income, education, and housing between Southern rural whites and Negroes." While numerically more Southern whites are classified as poor, the black poverty is universally worse by any measure—dollar income, housing, health services, education, and on and on. As the commission observes: "Although many poor white families are found in Southern states, the deprivation among Negroes is especially intense." Still, it may come as some surprise that in a total Southern head count of the poverty-stricken more whites than blacks are numbered, despite any racial gradations of need. But here the facts of this century's epochal black migration from the South color the tabulations. In this region where blacks comprised roughly half the population before the Civil War, whites now outnumber them better than four to one. And the ratio is increasing. The political implications in this are generally overlooked but they help make understandable the unrelenting white pressures on blacks to move out. Despite the Voting Rights Act of 1965 and the resultant extraordinary increase of black voters in the eleven Southern states that went from roughly two million in 1964 to three million in 1968, Negroes generally lack the numbers to exert any significant control at local levels, where decisions on taxes, schools, police, and other vital areas of life are made. For example, in the five Deep South states of Alabama, Georgia, Mississippi, Louisiana, and South Carolina, with a total of 418 counties, Negroes have a *potential* voting majority in only 65 counties and have achieved it through registration in only a dozen of these. Black migration ensures that these figures will never markedly improve, and so the poverty that induces migration is a key factor in the calculations of white politicians determined that the old order in Dixie will not be changed.

In 1964, before the hope of the civil rights movement gave way to disillusion and racial grief expressed in violence, the Reverend C. T. Vivian of the Southern Christian Leadership Conference addressed a crowd of Negroes in St. Augustine, Florida, surrounded by jeering whites. The Reverend Vivian cried out into the tense night:

"We don't say take away jobs from anybody. We say, let everybody have better jobs, Negroes included, poor whites included. All of us. For God's sake, we all need more in this Southland. They say Negroes steal. Yet segregation takes thirty billion dollars a year from Negroes and other minorities. With that thirty billion we could see the Southland flower as it's supposed to be. The thievery has come from higher up, from the system of segregation itself. For you see, if we were really inferior, there wouldn't have to be a system of segregation to keep us down because we wouldn't be able to aspire. My God, what kind of people can there be that break a man's leg and then blame him because he limps?"

Vivian's cry has a forlorn echo four years later. The Movement in the South succeeded in creating motion here and there, progress in one city or another. But in vast rural sections it has turned into a wheel spinning in a clay road, whirling around, futilely seeking traction, a big black wheel going nowhere. Buck Sims and tens of thousands like him are worse off today than five years ago, driven from the land, their only monuments bare chimney stacks that once had been hearths standing in fields where once had been cotton. When they knock on the gates of Southern factories, they are likely to be offered a broom and a janitor's job, or turned away. The U.S. Civil Rights Commission, surveying job discrimination in Alabama during 1968, found rampant evidence of unequal treatment of blacks in mill and factory. August corporate names like American Can and Dan River Mills were discovered to be only in "paper compliance" with federal job equality laws. Such firms held millions of dollars' worth of federal contracts which *must* be canceled if discrimination persists. But civil rights law is a sometime thing.

In neither Alabama nor anywhere in the Deep South, nor any-where in the entire United States, *has a single federal contract been canceled because a company is not complying with the law of the land barring discrimination.*

Poor whites who would not stand with blacks in a brother-hood (at least) of need are surviving in better style. But "better" is only relative to "worse." Compared to the American "aver-age," many of these white lives would inspire appeals for Wash-ington foreign aid were they being lived overseas. They are lives circumscribed by poverty that forces the son of an illiterate father to quit school at fourteen, assuring the perpetuation of ignorance with all its material and spiritual cripplers. There are not many white bellies swollen with hunger in the South but there are rickety minds beyond number. Starved for nour-ishment they do not know they lack, these white lives languish in mill towns, on hardscrabble farms, or in the hills of Appa-lachia, like dogs consigned to the cold thresholds of doors open-ing on warmth. How can we explain them while we boast the world's highest standard of living except to admit that we have the world's highest tolerance of indifference?

Because the evidence of indifference is everywhere despite a mass ("maze" is probably more accurate) of government pro-grams assertedly designed to eliminate poverty whatever the color and to insure equal opportunity for all.[11] The Office of Economic Opportunity, the Department of Health, Education and Welfare, the Departments of Interior and of Labor—all publish handsome and expensive brochures telling what they do to improve the lot of America's downtrodden.[12] But the ob-scene truth is they do so little—and that so selectively—that logic dictates the conclusion that the national intent is to create the illusion of basic change while letting the reality of need persist.

Officials of the Southern Regional Council and I felt that these realities should be plainly identified. In the summer of 1967, I visited the states of Georgia, South Carolina, Kentucky, Florida, and Alabama, moving among the poor, listening to their stories, trying to learn the facts of poverty. The survey does not claim to be scientific. I try to sketch some patterns of pri-vate and governmental conduct that have created poverty and now are institutionalizing it. You can knock on any shack door and find a tale of woe to touch the heart; but this is merely an exercise in pathos unless cause is marked along with effect. Current journalism, while producing sympathetic and evocative descriptions of the plight of Southern poor, invariably oversimplifies the cause and distorts reality. It is common to see the blame placed on farm mechanization, which has eliminated field jobs. This *is* a factor in the worsening Southern rural environment. But people went hungry, shacks sagged, babies died as they began life, and minds languished in ignorance long before the first tractor rumbled into the cotton fields. It may relieve the conscience to place the blame on a machine. But poverty in the South or anywhere else isn't that simple.

The people and institutions that help to create poverty would have us believe it is simple, simply the case of shiftless persons with too many children, too little brains, too black, too trashy. Clearly, all the poor aren't wise and noble; but neither are all those with a sufficiency. There exist poverty-making mechanisms beyond the powers of the individual to control. Efforts to identify them become technical, even tedious. In the South there are complexities of acreage allotments, soil bank checks, school curricula, mill and mine ownership, and the damnable factor of racism weaving through all. But the effort must be made. No one ever expects to cure cancer by merely weeping over the victim or slipping him a placebo; yet this is the prevailing therapeutic approach America generally takes to poverty.

Having said all that, promising a cool and analytical treatment of the subject, a modifier of emotionality is filed. The raw material of the subject is people. And these people, physically dispossessed from the land or socially and economically evicted from the American society of plenty, are emotion-laden.

"You don't know where your trouble is comin' from," said a Negro mother in Lee County, Georgia. "But you know it's comin'."

And it comes. To black hands pulling white cotton for the profit of the Man, to white hands clawing black coal for the profit of the Man. It comes most often and hardest to those who break poverty's first law of survival: don't get old and don't get sick; and the second: don't get pregnant. Maybe that should be the first. There is nothing harder than for a parent

who perceives that education may give his child the salvation
denied him to watch that child drop from school because he
has to work or because some lessons never written in a primer
are just too hard to learn.

"They call me a nigger," said Leo Roy, a Negro trying to
make it in Alabama's desegregated Choctaw County High
School. "The white kids call me a dirty, stinky swamp rat."

Traveling a South blessed with beauty and cursed with
racism, poor where it should prosper and too often hoarding
its prosperity inside artificial lines of city or county while
neighbors want, the traveler still sees patches of hope. There
are federal programs that could work if Washington and the
states had the will and provided the resources to work them.
There are rural people coming together in cooperatives latent
with promise. There are sprouts of brotherhood, tough and
tender with awakened Christianity, pushing up in what used to
be a wasteland of racial arrogance. In so many ways it is a saner,
healthier, more solvent region than it was in the thirties when
W. L. Cash could write on the last page of his monumental
The Mind of the South:

> Violence, intolerance, aversion and suspicion toward new ideas,
> an incapacity for analysis, an inclination to act from feeling
> rather than from thought, an exaggerated individualism and a
> too narrow concept of social responsibility, attachment to fictions
> and false values, above all too great attachment to racial values
> and a tendency to justify cruelty and injustice in the name of
> those values—these have been its characteristic vices in the past.
> And, despite changes for the better, they remain its characteristic
> vices today.

The South is better, but the forces that thwarted progress for
so long are sweeping forward again. They do not care that land
with resources capable of supporting all is filling with black
peasants denied the chance to support themselves and white
expendables treated like trash and becoming what they have
been ordained to be. These forces gloat over Northern racial
hypocrisy finally and fully revealed while they stoke the fires
of Newark and Detroit by privately looting black generations
of money and manhood, then strut their moral outrage when

looted migrants publicly loot the North.[13] They damn even feeble federal help to Southern poor and obstruct home-grown efforts to alleviate poverty.[14]

"My God," asked the Reverend Vivian, "what kind of people can there be that would break a man's leg and then blame him because he limps?"

How the crippled endure, eke out their meager store of hope, and strive to prevail against the forces crippling them will be a recurrent theme in these pages.

3

"Charlie: This letter is to advise you . . ."

HOW does a man like Buck Sims learn that he is all through?
He receives a letter of eviction similar to the following, which
came to a neighbor of his in Greene County. The names have
been changed, but the dates are actual and they are interesting.

MAY 21, 1966

CARTER ROBERTS,

Our mother, Mrs. Hannah McNeil, did not know when she
rented the house to you that we do not wish to rent the house at
this time. We ask you to vacate the house by June 1, 1966.

MISS ALMA MCNEIL
MRS. DOAK WALTERS
MRS. GROVER CHAPMAN

Here is another familiar to Alabama Negro tenant farmers;
this time the county is Sumter, just below Greene. The dates
also tell a story. This was a form letter received by many
farmers, the names and addresses typed in.

Nov. 25, 1966

CHARLIE WHITE
ROUTE 2, BOX 80
PANOLA, ALABAMA

CHARLIE:

This letter is to advise you that the land which you have been
renting from me for the past several years will no longer be

available to you for rent. I have rented this land to —— Paper Co. and they are going to grow timber on the lands.

This is to give you notice that you will not be able to have the acreage formerly cultivated by you, for the years 1967 and thereafter, and you can make arrangements to get acreage elsewhere.

If you wish to live in the house which you have occupied, you can continue to do so for a monthly rental of $15. The first rent payment will be due on or before the 5th day of January, 1967.

Under my contract with the paper company, you will not be able to have a garden or any cultivable land, or have any pasture or run any livestock, nor will you be able to cut any wood from the woods.

This is to advise you that if you do not wish to rent the house, then you must immediately make your arrangements to vacate the property before January 1, 1967, when the —— Paper Co. will take charge of the property.

Yours very truly,

MRS. DEBORAH CALHOUN

It was one month before Christmas when Charlie—addressed by his first name like a child to make certain there could be no confusion between him and a man meriting Christian consideration—received this classic letter. Charlie White was given five weeks in dead of winter to decide where he would go, what he would do to live now that he had no land, how his family would eat.[15] Carter Roberts was given only ten days. But then, his notice came in spring and it soon would be summertime, when the livin' is easy.

How many tenants have been turned out like animals in Alabama and elsewhere no one knows. Evictees are the most powerless and thus discountable segment of the disintegrating body of Negro farmers whose total has fallen from 926,000 in 1920 to an estimated 180,000 in 1964 (all but one percent residing in the South).[16] Tenants have no legal protection against peremptory eviction; a city slum dweller has safeguards against being turned out into the street, agencies to help him if he is destitute, but a tenant can overnight be ordered off land he has farmed for years. The Department of Agriculture demonstrates virtually no interest in their plight (and the attendant drift of the landless into cities) beyond outbursts of rhetoric.[17]

Why tenants are being turned out involves a variety of reasons. Landowners in western Alabama say variously that they can make more money from timber or soybeans on land Negro tenants historically farmed in corn, peanuts, or that old dollar standby cotton. They say that most of the Negro operators were getting too old to farm profitably. The first is possibly true; the second undeniable, given the immemorial role of black farmers in Southern agriculture that guaranteed most would be broke and exhausted at fifty, scratching at small, unprofitable parcels of bleached-out soil.[18] The age of Negro farmers reflects the tragic mistiming of the civil rights movement in the South, begun after migration had sapped much young black strength from rural areas. A few decades earlier, had the youth and vigor of great numbers of Negroes still on the land been inspired to action, a new Southern order might have been created. But that is another story. . . .

The landowner's rationale that "his" Negroes were getting too old to farm seemingly denied that supposed symbiotic relationship wherein black and white, in roles of serf and liege, worked out their mutual survival. Did those prior years of symbiosis count for nothing? Eskimos, it is said, put their aged on ice floes to die. The tenant is left at the side of the road, eviction notice in hand. Are profit and age the only considerations in his abandonment to penury?

There are other considerations. There is civil rights activity, which, fully realized, must reveal the old relationship for what it is—black trading manhood for a variable handout, white cloaking exploitation in robes of charity—and having revealed it, must destroy it. The threat of change outrages white emotion. One evicted farmer gave this testimony to a Justice Department listener who inquired during a voting rights investigation of the farmer's relationship to Mr. Charlie:

"There wasn't a better man to work for. Me and him worked five years. But since this redishin' [registering] he been like a wild man. He been pushin' me, treatin' me mean. Then day after election he come to the window an' said, 'Get out of that house by sundown or I'll tear the roof off it.' "

And still other, more calculated, considerations. These involve the Agriculture Department's Agriculture Stabilization and Conservation Service (ASCS), in particular its program that pays farmers to divert land from cotton production. The role of cotton in the American economy is extremely complex; its monetary importance is indicated by a federal subsidy to the industry of about a billion dollars a year and the fact that cotton exports are the biggest single source of U.S. foreign exchange. The department has tried many schemes to balance production with marketability. Almost without exception, these schemes extract prohibitive penalties on the poor, small farmer and often drive him off the land. For example, a landowner with a 5,000-acre plantation can absorb a 10 percent cutback in his acreage allotment and survive grumbling; to a man with only four or five acres in cotton figured to the last penny, it could mean disaster. The principle of the graduated income tax, where the least are assessed the least, seemingly should apply to cotton allotments. It doesn't because the Department of Agriculture is geared to the marketing needs of big operators despite all its pious disclaimers. In 1966, *one* single big operation received $2.8 million in federal subsidies. The President's Advisory Council on Rural Poverty reported that the poorest 10 percent of the nation's cotton farmers received only 1 percent of federal benefits, while the richest 10 percent were paid *50* percent of the cotton benefits.

Compounding this problem in the Black Belt is Agriculture's sorry role as a silent partner in prejudice.[19] In 1965, the U.S. Civil Rights Commission bluntly charged USDA with practicing discrimination. Three years later, in 1968, the commission investigating Agriculture programs in Alabama found "no significant change." Implementation of ASCS programs like cotton diversion is left to county committees, which allocate vast federal funds. These three-man ASCS committees wield make-or-break farming power [20] and in theory are democratically controlled through community elections in which all farmers—owners and tenants—cast equal ballots. In practice, these elections over the decades have been as fraudulent and racially unrepresentative as most Deep South civil elections. The pernicious old combinations of guile, intimidation, and ignorance have worked to the detriment of Negro farmers who were disenfranchised in dozens of ways from voting for county committeemen who would truly represent them. As we shall see, this is one of the major causes of black poverty in the rural South—abuses tolerated and encouraged by the Department of Agriculture that range from barring Negro *children* from 4-H Club activities to withholding acreage allotments from Negroes.[21] Proof that black farmers are denied access to the elections that produce the all-important three-man county committees is visible in these figures: there are 58 counties in the South where Negro farmers outnumber whites. There are 320 counties where Negro farmers comprise 20 percent or more of farm operators. Through 1967, *not a single Negro served on a single county committee in the entire South.*[22] Poverty is not simple.

Belated directives from the White House and Secretary Freeman have brought some token improvement, although the retroactive loss to Negro farmers can never be made up. Which brings us back to the evictees and the question of the cotton diversion checks. Farmers who voluntarily plant less cotton than they are allotted receive federal cash payments and loan benefits. Under the law, owners are prohibited from putting tenants off the land in order to retire cotton fields and collect benefits. The law also says that tenants are supposed to collect for acres they have rented that are "diverted." In practice, the misappropriation of these checks is a Black Belt scandal of multimillion-dollar proportions. Over the years, ignorant and intimidated black tenants—and some whites—have not received their portion. Some assigned their checks to the owner, trusting his accounting to square with them after tenant debts were deducted. Thousands of others simply never saw the checks, which were mailed by the county committees to the landowners, cashed, and the money pocketed by someone. The otherwise excellent Civil Rights Commission report makes no mention of this, and a spokesman for Agriculture brought to mind the joke about the fox guarding the henhouse when he said it was up to the ASCS committees to "see that an equal sharing was made."

However, the Movement stirred some tenants in Sumter County to inquire about those ASCS checks, to demand that checks be mailed to *them* rather than to the Man. Charlie

White, evicted before Christmas in Panola, was among them. He went to the landowner's agent to discuss the payment form.

"He talked in a way like we was goin' to get the money," White says. "But I didn't believe he was tellin' me the truth. I started readin' the form an' he reached over an' grabbed it back." [23]

For his temerity, White received an eviction notice instead of a check.[24] Eventually, the NAACP sent money and legal help into Sumter County, and some of the tenants were allowed to pay rent on the shacks for another year, provided they did not put a seed in the soil, or burn a branch from the woods, or put a shoat in a pen. How Charlie White would eat in a county without food programs was his business since no one from Washington to the county seat in Panola clearly gave a damn.

4

What They Really Want

WHAT is it like when a tenant doesn't even get the reprieve of a rented shack roof over his head? Before Buck Sims passes from these pages into whatever oblivion awaits him, he has a story to tell. He stands outside a small Negro general store and café on Highway 80, Greene County, the air pungent with the smell of barbecue cooking over charcoal in back. Sims is neatly turned out in a clean, open-necked white shirt, pressed black trousers, and a wide-brimmed hat of a Western style favored in Alabama. With him is an acquaintance, a farmer named Lewis Hood, who still has a place, and Mrs. Sims. She holds the grandchild left by the daughter buried on Dick Silver Hill. The baby's name is Julia Ann; she has a three-year-old sister. Mrs. Sims is in her late forties, a rather handsome woman in a white and red checked cotton dress, freshly ironed. During the conversation in the hot sun the baby never cries and the grandmother never smiles.

"It's just pitiful," she says. "I just kinda need help an' I can't get it. This child needs milk all the time but there's many a time she don't get it. We're eatin' okry an' peas every day. It's no way to live. An' we're not newcomers. We been here a time. You saw those graves up on the hill?"

"We got the eviction letter at the end of '64," her husband says. "I never knowed why. You got no way of findin' out the reason but you can see them puttin' the land in soybeans. We always gave 'em rent in advance, I can say that. Course, my brothers an' me had been in civil rights but some that hadn't been was turned out too. Altogether from our farm there was eight families an' twelve from the place above had to get out. They cut my brother Hampton's allotment altogether that year, never give a reason, then turned him loose in the winter with nine kids. They lived in the colored schoolhouse or I don't know where they would have lived. A friend lent me a shack he had. He meant to help but it was worse than nothin'. I sent a letter to the Justice Department about gettin' put out but I never heard nothin' from them. An' there was families livin' down by the swamp slow to get out because they had no place to go. So the white folks went in one day with bulldozers, knocked down the houses an' barns, then set fire to it all with the belongin's inside."

A listener is reminded of *The Grapes of Wrath* and the bull-dozer operators sent out by Eastern banks foreclosing farm mort-gages, bulldozers churning dust clouds, the masked and goggled drivers looming like robots as they demolished the houses of the Okies. It was white farmers then, thirty years ago, who learned that to plow the land, seed it, wait with it for rain and sun, and gather its sometime yield gave you no claim beyond papers drawn in a law office. Buck Sims had, in titular regard, less claim than the Okies. The deed had never even been his. But what knowledge of the law acknowledged, something else denied. Didn't the Sims graveyard constitute a statute, convey a right of occupancy which men had lived and died for five generations to establish?

"That old shack was so bad," says Mrs. Sims, shifting the baby from one arm to the other, "that when SNCC brought in three tents, we went to live in them. But can you imagine, after living your life in a house and raising your children to have to go live in a tent at my age? No water, no toilet, dirt for a floor. And cold. What I want to know is, who says people should have to live like that?"

Mrs. Sims' anger at her woman's humiliation is not forced, on display for a white listener. It covers her like her skin. It is what she is. She makes no bid for sympathy; she does not once mention the daughter who died in the tent. She does not talk about the ASCS, crop allotments, or the relative merits of soybeans and cotton. But in a few words, she summons indignant images of hands warming at a kerosene stove while shadows huddle against canvas bellying in a rain.

"The Movement helped with milk an' the money to buy food," her husband continues. "Welfare wouldn't give nothin' because they said I could work.[25] Which I could if there *was* work or land to work on. The tents went bad, sprung leaks. One burnt down in a stove fire. After our baby died we wanted to go. An' she died of the cold, remember that. We got to live in a 'bandoned shack on colored land an' that's where we are now."

Sims paused and stood looking at Highway 80 in the practiced attitude of a man who has not had much to do for a long while but stand around watching the cars go by. It is a Southern syndrome.

"Never took a day of charity in my life," Sims says. "But it's like this: they cut out the commodities here an' put in stamps. We been gettin' forty-eight dollars' worth for eight dollars. If it wasn't for the stamps a whole lot of people couldn't eat. But they don't hardly last two weeks. Then you gotta scuffle it up somehow, you just scrape aroun'. Sometimes I get a little luck an' make a day or two as a mechanic or yardman. Pays eight dollars. But you can't see no way ahead. Even those still got land can't hardly make it between the 'lotments they give you an' the Man squeezin' all the time."

"Can't lie about that," says Lewis Hood. He is about fifty, sinewy, taking care of a wife, son, and five grandchildren. Before stamp prices were cut in midsummer under pressure of unfavorable publicity, he had been paying $40 for $70 worth of stamps for himself, wife, and son. When the grandchildren arrived down from the North, he was told that for eight persons he would have to pay $42 in exchange for $98 worth of stamps. It seems fair enough, and may be, if you have the extra $2. Hood didn't, and so he continued on the old three-person allotment.

"I once had ten acres in cotton when Bill Williams, a colored man, owned the land," continues Hood. "Then it was sold and the allotment went down to six acres split between me and another farmer. In 1967 it was cut to three for the entire spread.

I went to the ASCS to protest and was told that 'lotments from the state was going to California." [26]

"Yeah," says Sims. "California. It used to be easier here years ago. You could raise hogs, keep a milk cow, can greens from the garden. I remember my granddaddy had three or four brood sows. He'd leave 'em right in the swamp off Dick Silver Hill an' when he wanted meat he'd call the sows by name. They'd come up with the shoats that'd been born on the farm. But those born in the swamp wouldn't come. When I was young I'd take a gun down there for the Fourth of July barbecue we had an' kill me a wild hog. No more.

"The old way you always had somethin' to sell or put aside. When you had a few dollars as a tenant, you had some kind of independence, you didn't have to beg—though no matter what you made off cotton you never saw it. My last crop in '64 I had nine acres makin' almost a bale to the acre at one hundred and fifty dollars a bale. But with what they sell fertilizer so high an' what they steal at the gin, I didn't realize a cent of money from the sale. Between boll weevil and bale weevil, it's hard to make money off cotton.

"Then the Man started tightenin' up in the fifties till the way they do it now you got your finger in the barrel an' you gotta play quiet till you get it out. They say, 'I don't want them cows rubbin' on my trees.' So you can't keep cows. They say, 'I don't want them hogs rootin' up my ground.' So you can't keep hogs. But what they really mean is they don't want you to have nothin' so when they come an' say, 'Work for me today for what I want to pay you,' you have to do it. Not for you to have nothin', that's what they really want."

5

Why Did Secretary Freeman Visit Herdis Jones?

AS evicted families and tenants still on the land struggled in the complex of rural poverty, Secretary of Agriculture Freeman visited western Alabama on one of his "town and country tours." It was a whirlwind affair—chartered buses zooming importantly along rural roads with natives left gaping in the exhaust, television crews running sweat-stained to record a handshake for posterity, bureaucratic underlings trying to look significant as they handed out press releases. One quoted Secretary Freeman on the purpose of the tour, which was covering not only Alabama but Iowa, Mississippi, and Indiana—all in four days, including travel time.

"We want to find out how federal programs are working outside the nation's big cities," the Secretary said. "I am a strong believer in close communication between citizens and public servants."

Planning the Alabama phase of the tour had created all sorts of agonizing appraisals and reappraisals over how Freeman should balance his "communication" between whites and Negroes. When the final itinerary indicated that he was not going to stop and talk to a group of desperate black farmers in Eutaw, word was conveyed to his staff that unless he stopped, the entourage would be embarrassed by a black roadblock.

Freeman stopped at a church meeting in Eutaw. But not for

long.[27] In Demopolis, there was time for luncheon with all-white business and civic leaders while Mrs. Freeman went on a "beautification" tour with the Demopolis Garden Clubs, visiting the historical plantation residence Gaineswood. It had been known that both occasions would conform to Demopolis segregationist practices.[28] Freeman did visit a Negro grocery store to see how the food stamp program was getting on. But for a man who had said it was "vitally important that I know what rural Americans are thinking," he somehow missed some typical rural Americans.

There were scores of men like Carter Roberts, Charlie White, and Buck Sims available to tell what happens to families when land is yanked out from under them. Scores like Lewis Hood watching a cotton allotment shrink from ten acres to six to three, and wondering whether they next would be allotting individual plants. There were disintegrating shacks to be visited right on the main road or back on isolated farms where the principal product, unlisted in Department of Agriculture production statistics, is misery. Then why did Secretary Freeman on his fact-finding mission descend on the stout cinder-block house of Herdis Jones, a former coal miner and present-day laborer on a white man's farm, Herdis Jones who had not worked on a tenant farm since he was a boy fifty years ago?

"I don't know," Jones told a visitor a month after Freeman came through. "They just slipped out on me. I don't even know, suh, exactly what Mr. Freeman is in charge of. Now he did ask me about the food stamps, how much I was gettin' an' I told him I liked them fine. Except any time I make a little extra they raise the price so that sets you right back where you were. But workin' as a tenant farmer in this part of the country isn't for me. When somebody else is usin' the pencil here, you're just workin' an' slavin' for nothin' because it never comes out right. He didn't ask me nothin' about that. But I could've told him. Everybody knows it."

Mrs. Jones sat barefoot beside her husband on rickety chairs on the shady side of the house, where a basketball hoop of baling wire was fastened to a log pole at the edge of a soybean field, the field's bright green stretching off like an undulant sea swell in the sun. Mrs. Jones was around fifty and thin; but she wore tiny gold earrings and eyeglasses glamorized by black-and-white plastic insets on the frames, and there was a perkiness about her not often encountered among the worked-out wives of black tenant farmers.

"I pick, yes Lord," she said. "But only in the fall when it gets cool. Some of the children too. There's a couple can do two hundred pounds a day. There's four dollars an' that helps. We all chop at two dollars a day but I'm gettin' too old for that in the heat an' all. Food? We gets enough food. The children, they eats till they leaves it. But if they cut out the food stamps"— Mrs. Jones laughed—"I'd just have to do the best I could."

Outriders from the Agriculture Department had "surveyed" Mr. and Mrs. Jones a few weeks before the tour. They found a Negro rural family that for a long while had lived an atypical city life. Jones, fifty-four, had worked in the mines outside Birmingham at good pay until the mines began closing in 1958. Then he returned to Greene County to drive a tractor at day rates for a Norwegian-born white man who has 125 acres in cotton and more than that in soybeans. In farming months, Jones said, he averaged $200 driving tractor at $1 an hour, the highest rate in Alabama. In the winter he made $50 a month caring for the man's cattle. Mr. and Mrs. Jones were not getting rich on this income but they had been getting by, even when he broke the first rule of the poor and took sick with bleeding ulcers.

"I was feelin' poor as a snake three months ago," he said. "I went to the county welfare doctor, an' he wrote out a script for the spells. It cost $14 at the drugstore, which I didn't have. I brought it back to welfare an' they said they paid for the doctor but not for the script. Lap-legged as I was, there wasn't nothin' to do but borrow it. We used to have a good doctor in the welfare who would help you with somethin' like that but he took sick hisself an' the new one don't listen to you."

The vagaries of welfare weren't the concern of Secretary Freeman. But things like the State Extension Service, about 50 percent financed by the federal government, were. The Extension Service is supposed to offer nondiscriminatory programs ranging from crop counseling through 4-H Clubs and home-making. Does it?

"I never in my life have seen nobody from the county agent office," Jones said. "I doubt if any other colored man aroun' here has either. But I can't say that for sure. I wrote 'em once about gettin' some home cannin' information an' they sent back a pamphlet. I still got the envelope here."

The envelope, from the Cooperative Extension Service, USDA, Auburn University, was addressed to "Herdis Jones" without the courtesy title of "Mr."

"Nobody roun' here calls a colored man Mistuh," Jones said with a tolerant smile for the visitor's question about it. "Un-lest he's a white man from out of town like some of the people come through with—what did you say the name was—Freeman? Mr. Freeman."

Had Mr. Freeman asked about discrimination in the Extension Service? [29]

"No, suh," Jones said. "He didn't ask nothin' at all about that. But the only thing I know to make things better aroun' here is to give everybody an equal chance. Now I don't have it too hard myself with the man what owns this place. He gets a little fractious sometimes but as long as he pays good I let him run right on. Meg here"—he reached over and patted his wife's knee—"she was all over in the Movement but the boss didn't care. He don't care about what colored folks do an' I don't hide nothin' from him. He'd come an' toot his horn in the mornin' an' I'd say I was goin' to redish or vote, an' he'd say, O.K., an' drive on."

Clearly, Secretary Freeman had encountered an unusual rural Alabama Negro family. But, equally clear, this had not happened by chance, since department scouts had marked the family for the visit, Freeman and Jones to stand chatting for the cameramen outside the cinder-block house, reporters to make appraisals in ten or fifteen minutes before the caravan moved on, certain questions to be asked officially and others neglected. The Jones family was not the exemplification of the American Dream in 1967 with Mrs. Jones, a grandmother four times over, still picking cotton and Mr. Jones scrounging to buy medicine. Still, they were getting enough to eat and you couldn't see the sky through their ceiling. And they were, after all, black. So it was a comforting impression left by the visit that things in western Alabama weren't so bad as they might be among the myriad unvisited Negro families who were, one was left to assume, keeping up with the Joneses.

6

"He's No Daddy of Mine"

"DID you have any breakfast today, Joseph?"

"No, suh," answers the twelve-year-old. He is a spindly brown boy with a light voice and quick eyes, walking barefoot on the Tuscaloosa sidewalk, occasionally leaving a dab of blood from his right foot. It was cut deep on the bottom five days ago and the unbandaged wound is festering and will not close.

"What about lunch?"

"Suh?"

"Did you have any lunch?"

"No, suh. But I believe we'll have some beans tonight."

"What about breakfast yesterday?"

"We didn't eat no breakfast yesterday. But that ain't all the time. It just happens sometimes. Sometimes we have jelly an' peanut butter. Sometimes baloney an' grits."

"Did your mama take you to a doctor about your foot?"

"No, suh. We ain't got no doctor. Onliest time I been to a doctor was when I got hit by a car an' it busted up my arm. It's all right now though."

"It looks good and strong. Do you play any sports?"

"Suh?"

"Do you like to play baseball or any games like that?"

"No, suh. But I like to ride a bike. That's what I want for Christmas. A bike."

"What did you get last Christmas?"

"Didn't get nothin'. But I'm fixin' to get a bike this Christmas."

"I understand you come from a big family. It must be hard for your mama to buy toys for everybody. How many brothers and sisters do you have?"

"I don't know, suh. Ten or twelve."

[The Reverend Francis Walter, whose Selma Inter-religious Project office is nearby, had prepared the visitor for Joseph Wilcox' uncertain arithmetic in a family where "husbands" come and go by recounting a conversation he recently overheard between two of Joseph's brothers.

First brother: Charley was by before.

Second: Who's that?

First: That's our daddy.

Second: That might be your daddy, but he's no daddy of mine.]

Exchanging pleasantries, the visitor and Joseph walk down the warm midafternoon street in the colored section toward his house, passing en route the Negro funeral home. It is a handsome frame-and-brick building, the best in a neighborhood of modest but not shacky houses, and there is a black limousine gleaming at the curbside. Joseph's shorts are splattered with white paint; he has been helping to paint the funeral home garage. Joseph likes the sedately prosperous atmosphere of the place and he confides his ambition at twelve: he wants to work in a funeral home when he grows up.

It seems an odd choice to his adult companion, who remembers the dread surrounding death at twelve, the frightful fascination of the doggerel song:

> Whenever you see the hearse roll by,
> Do you sometimes think you're going to die,
> And the worms crawl in, the worms crawl out . . .

Odd until Joseph turns off the sidewalk down an alley to his house. The sound of children crying fills the ears; the nose fills with a stench of urine and garbage and undefinable odors of decay. There is a dirt yard, running with small children and littered with the kitchen midden of poverty: Royal Crown Cola caps, treadless car tires, fish bones, watermelon rinds, scraps of cloth, clots of paper, decomposing animal and human offal. There is a house, a shack, a hut, a habitation of time-darkened boards leaning together for support. In the yard sits an old black man, his eyes cloudy with cataracts, a switch in his hand. The youngest children, up to three or four, are naked and the rest wear combinations of clothes and rags. One girl holds an infant clad in a diaper that once, a good while ago, had been fresh. A few of the children are simply standing as if caught in the childhood game of "Freeze!" Their faces are torpid, their eyes look entranced. Others run around, deliberately scooting past the old man, who is their grandfather.

"Come run by my feet again, I'll get you," he says, flicking the switch and turning his head toward what he can see only dimly. A boy about two stumbles by the old man's feet and the grandfather whips him. The boy yowls and squirms out of reach, wailing. Two others take up the wail and, for no discernible reason, begin hitting out at each other, striking bitterly with their inconsequential fists.

[A Negro girl, Pat Brown, working in the Inter-religious Project office, had involved herself with the Wilcox family. It was just another case, she said, of black drift from farm into city, people coming from need unprepared for even more rigorous urban demands, the grandfather once a cropper, then a tenant, finally urban flotsam washed up by Southern tidal surges.[30] Black frustration, she said, flowed thicker than blood through family veins, and members were diseased by self-hate, suffering rages of love and fear.

"I've seen the grandmother beating one of the little girls," Miss Brown said. "I mean, really beating her. But the girl held onto her while she got beat, wouldn't let her go, crying and holding on. Just like that was all there was to hold onto."]

Joseph's mother is leaving for work as he arrives.[31] She is a cook in a white restaurant, a stout woman whose spotlessly clean and scrupulously starched work uniform is in gleaming contrast to the surroundings. She has to hurry and in any event is not anxious to answer the prying inquiries of a total stranger who has grown accustomed to the generosity of the poor in sharing their one considerable possession, the material facts of their life. Nine of the children are hers; two others are somebody's; there is no husband in the picture. She works six days a week in the restaurant and makes $28; *her* mother works as a domestic and in a sandwich shop, averaging about the same. Welfare gives $91 a month in aid to dependent children which, under Alabama law, can be cut off if she stops working. The house costs $30 a month, light $5; there are no commodities or food stamps so groceries take everything else—she has to run now.

Joseph leads the way into the house, brothers and sisters trailing tentatively. The rooms are boxes of half-light with corners of darkness. The air is acid with the smell of urine soaked into mattresses without sheets, the ticking splotched with stains superimposed on each other, some of the largest possibly from the birth of children, all delivered at home. Mrs. Wilcox and three children sleep in one bed, four children in another, two more here, the grandparents somewhere. There are only four rooms counting the kitchen, each about 10 feet by 10 feet, and there are no closets. Clothing is piled in corners on the floor. There are no chairs, no tables, no lamps; dark thresholds lead from one windowless box to the next.

There *is* a window in the kitchen, screen dangling, and flies have been alert to a good thing. They cover the wood stove, where (Joseph had guessed right) a pot of beans with neck bones simmers beside a fly-glazed tin of cornbread. The smell of the beans is almost canceled by a stench of smoke, grease, and damp sweating out of the walls. Plates in the kitchen can be counted—two—but roaches run beyond computation. There is an electric refrigerator containing a bunch of wilted mustard greens; the greens have the refrigerator to themselves. A cot is placed along one wall and the visitor assumes, in the absence of table and chairs, that it is there to eat on. But Joseph explains that it is the bed of his eldest sister, sixteen, who is permitted to sleep alone. Questions arise in the musty confinement of the rooms. How do people wash or bathe? There is no inside water, only a pump in the yard near a forbidding outhouse. There can be no privacy, the word itself may lack meaning anymore to the Wilcoxes in their claustrophobic environment where flesh is continually brushing flesh in fetid dark. How do the children of school age do homework without tables or desks on which to write, without quiet space in which to think, without all the gracious elements that go into the rosy American image of children receiving the best education that a free society with the world's highest standard of living can offer.

("The children go to school once or twice a week," Pat Brown said. "The mother just can't cope, and the authorities permit it to happen. Like with his foot. There's a clinic service available for emergencies and checkups but she just won't take them. Nobody ever checks up on the children so they just do like they're doing. Reverend Walter took an interest and bought memberships in the Y for Joseph and a couple of his brothers. Then they couldn't go because they lacked sneakers and sweatshirts. So he bought them. And so then the mother said No, they couldn't go because she heard once a child drowned in a swimming pool. Joseph is unusual because he's lasted bright for so long. Usually by his age this kind of living has lost it to them.")

Outside the house the air is thin enough to breathe. A reluctant good-bye is said to Joseph; it seems an act of abandonment to leave him there.

In his office, the Reverend Walter expresses Christian but not sanguine feelings about the Wilcox family. The condition of the elders, lamentable as it may be, can be accepted as an accomplished fact of life. But so many of the children already seem lost, and that is something else.

"There's an older brother, Julian, about fourteen," Reverend Walter says. "Julian's an arsonist. He used to come in here all the time like the others do, saying, 'Walter, I'm hungry, gimme some breakfast.' Then one day he set fire to the bathroom and almost burned us out. He went on setting others in the neighborhood and they picked him up and sent him away to the colored mental hospital at Searcy. There are five doctors there for two thousand five hundred Negro patients. None of the doctors is a psychiatrist and two don't even speak English. Do you think Julian will come back cured?" [32]

He shook his head, a young man alternately angry and anguished, dedicated to the project started in memory of seminarian Jonathan Daniels slain by an Alabama racist, but increasingly assailed by feelings of futility.

"If you're poor and black you'd better be strong," he says. "There's another brother arrested for putting sand in car gas tanks. He couldn't control his bladder in school and all his teachers said he was disturbed. He was supposed to have gotten psychological tests but he never did. He was very happy when he was picked up by the cops, to get all the attention he never got before. Now he's out on probation and it's only a matter of time before he does something else."

One despairing tale about the family follows another. There are almost laughable incongruities recalling the classic sociological stories of the thirties about the Jukes and the Kallikaks, poverty-stricken white mountain families, whose disordered lives were so gross that humorists eventually satirized them. The Reverend Walter tells of a student who tried to improve the Wilcox environment. He asked the children to help him gather all the refuse in the yard. They were puzzled but complied, and the student rented a truck and carted off the refuse. But the children promptly filled up the yard again, and proudly called him to see; they assumed he wanted the trash for some purpose they could not fathom.

It does not require a sociology degree to know that the Wilcox family is sick, morbidly sick, sick beyond the random efforts of the Reverend Walter and Miss Brown to make it well. The roots of its chaotic existence reach deep into white America's treatment of black. It is pointless, even cruel, to remonstrate that other Alabama Negroes handle their poverty with more style, that other mothers are better managers on the pittance that is their share of the nation's wealth.[33] Some would blame Mrs. Wilcox' plight on her sex life, with its careless production of children. But morality, like poverty, is not simple and the complexities in each are often intertwined. Movement preachers, answering the charge that black illegitimacy proves that Negroes were depraved, had a standard rejoinder: white women have abortions, black women have children.

There is truth in that and oversimplification too. White and black poor in the South and throughout America universally have more children than they can afford, although not more than the national income can afford. A life in utter poverty is lived outside the regulatory fiction of order self-imposed by a society that can own houses, send children to college, regularly see the doctor and dentist, and plan retirement income. It is a life intrinsically unstable and roundly ignorant. Men and women caught in it are, of course, no more sexually "good" or "bad" than their economic betters. Their natural impulses simply create bigger burdens, and what is done out of ignorance or carelessness can't be undone by a "therapeutic" abortion for a married woman, an extended trip to distant relatives by an unmarried girl. Fathers break and run under economic pressures. Mothers accept illegitimacy as a way of life. There are infinite gradations of moral responsibility and concern for the children, and if some mothers may be dismissed as depraved others must be lauded if they love to bring life into the world and stubbornly care for it under trying conditions. Newspapers and magazines delight in running pictures, particularly around Easter, of large, nicely dressed families, husband and wife smiling over an infant in arms while fifteen or twenty brothers and sisters fan out on either side. Why should this urge toward procreation, with its impulses profane and profound, be so attractive in the solvent and so heinous in the poor?

In the case of Mrs. Wilcox, an ancient national crime had been committed and if some of its racial victims survived better than others, this did not justify unconcern for those like her who languished. What kind of logic argues that, if two innocent men fall before an assailant's pistol and one makes a partial recovery from the wounds while the other lies paralyzed, the assailant has the right to be scornful of the paralyzed victim while demanding both forgiveness and loyalty from his almost-whole companion? The Wilcox family and others like it require total care, rehabilitation of their health, education, and living conditions if the lives of the children are to be saved. Some idea of the scope of black need may be gleaned from a report to the U.S. Civil Rights Commision in 1968 by Dr. Alan C. Mermann, assistant pediatrics professor at Yale Medical School. He surveyed health conditions in Lowndes County, Alabama, a few counties downstate from Tuscaloosa. Dr. Mermann reported that of 709 children studied, "eighty percent had anemia sufficient to require treatment in any doctor's office anywhere in the country. [But] ninety percent of the children said they had never seen a doctor. One of those who answered yes to the question said: 'Yes, he pulled my tooth.'

"... twenty-five percent of the children, one in four, needed further referral for glasses. One child out of the 709 I examined has glasses."

Dr. Mermann told the Civil Rights Commissioners that 80 percent of adults and children he examined "have approximately two-thirds of the amount of red blood [cells] that the commissioners have.

"This gives you some idea of the extent of fatigue," he said. "It explains, I think, some of the fatigue of the mother of six or eight children, some of the fatigue she has when she is operating on a very low margin of oxygen-carrying capacity in her blood. It explains the difficulty that a man might have in providing for his family. His inability to work on. This has a profound economic impact on the community involved."

The job of bringing twentieth-century diet and medicine to Lowndes and its myriad counterparts requires massive commitments. The only institution with the resources for the job is the federal government. The state of Alabama (or that collection of men and mores called a state) has demonstrated by a thousand sins of commission and omission that it does not choose to assume the responsibility, even if it has the resources. Men like the Reverend Walter and numerous private groups are trying to do the work of governments in arousing the poor, the dispossessed, the disenfranchised to press for their fair share of America. The federal government, by its fitful and insufficient measures, encourages this work, even makes it mandatory if anything is ever to be accomplished beyond legislative gestures. Many like the Reverend Walter put their personal ambitions in abeyance as they substitute for the government in a spirit epitomized by a poster in the Inter-religious Project office showing Christ on the Cross and beneath it the words:

> The figure of the crucified invalidates all
> thought which takes success as its standard

The sentiment of self-denial and human concern is a noble one. But too many of the dedicated bring only dedication to their labors; they aren't wise or experienced enough to make an impact even if they have adequate money and facilities. Some mesmerize themselves with their indignation at injustice, verbally lulling themselves into a state where the line between words and deeds grows indistinct, and the illusion of progress assumes substance. Others share the lot of the poor in the belief that living on grits and greens is an achievement of some kind, when mostly it is a self-satisfying exercise of their Christian ethic. My impulse is not to criticize them, since they at least are trying to involve themselves while the majority of their countrymen stand gawking at poverty like spectators watching a man run over by a car. But sometimes it is hard to be charitable, when observing, for example, a field worker for a project in western Alabama ask one black tenant after another if he would like the government to lend him money for a farm of his own, a nice brick house, modern equipment. It was playing a game of "if dreams came true" with people who had lived too long on dreaming.

The Reverend Walter is one of the capable ones and so he has no illusions about the scope of his achievements. He was chairman of the Advisory Committee to the Freedom Quilting Bee of Wilcox County.[34] Through sales of colorful homemade quilts sewn by poor ladies of the county, plus some loans and gifts, about $10,000 was realized in one year. The most made by any one of the 125 members, however, was $300, and with problems of distribution there was no guarantee this level would be maintained. The Reverend Walter had also been effectively active in the fight to get a $400,000 OEO grant for the fledgling Southwest Alabama Farmers Co-operative Association threatened by federal timidity in the face of rabid objections from Alabama officials.

"You have to go through such garbage just to get a crumb," he says. "For a kid like Joseph Wilcox you can't even get that. Washington says it wants to keep poor untrained Southerners from migrating to the Northern and Western big cities. In some cases a few hundred dollars a year cash income would keep them where they are. But Washington does little or nothing to provide it. I sometimes think the main purpose of these co-operatives may be to organize and train people for the coming revolution. I know that I have no firm rationale anymore."

7

*The Road to Joe Johnson's Place** *

IT begins symbolically crossing the Edmund Pettus Bridge from the west into Selma, Alabama. The Movement had once surged out of Selma, over the bridge in the opposite direction after a black man named Jimmy Lee Jackson and a white man name the Reverend James Reeb had been murdered in the quest for black self-realization and white atonement. Now, in midsummer of 1967, a pervasive quiet rises from the muddy Alabama River below. The sunny silence denies that some people ever sang freedom songs and others died here to change Selma. It is as if Selma were locked in an immemorial order that nothing had disturbed, or could.

The proper route to Joe Johnson's place is a right turn off the bridge down River Road, with its few remaining antebellum warehouses, the filigreed iron balconies reminiscent of New Orleans and recalling Selma's free-wheeling heyday befor the Civil War when traffic in slaves, bank notes, and sporting bloods made it the hottest little town on the river. But there is time for a roundabout drive, mixing memories of the recent past and present realities.

On broad Main Street, oversized cement flowerpots bearing bright blooms have been set out on the sidewalk along the length of the business district. One is in front of a music shop. A visitor recalls that on the day the marchers to Montgomery

---

* Joe Johnson is the tenant farmer who is chairman of the Southwest Alabama Farmers Co-operative Association (SWAFCA).

passed this shop, its public address system was playing at full tilt "Bye Bye Blackbird." The flowerpot calling customers to commerce has been placed there by Negro and white youths employed in the local Poverty Program. While Selma slums went unbeautified, this seemed a curious choice for the program's attentions, particularly in light of an OEO regulation stating: "No project may primarily or directly serve the financial interest of a private individual or profit-making organization."

The Poverty Program has not been a success in Selma, seat of Dallas County, although success was needed.[35] The failure has epitomized the post-Movement disillusion of many "militant" Southern Negroes who feel that all the march hurly-burly and the national legislation it inspired have changed the image of their place in the South but not its essence. The Dallas County OEO Community Action Program had become dominated by a coalition of white and Negro "moderates." (The words "militant" and "moderate," like most of our labels identifying left, right, and center, are so imprecise and subjective that they explain little. They only indicate a tone of thinking and this *may* be better than nothing in suggesting the true political color of thought.) The "moderate" Negroes included old-line leaders like Mrs. Amelia Boynton and the Reverend Frederick Reese. The "moderate" whites derived from the revamped power structure that had backed Wilson Baker in his successful campaign against former Sheriff Jim Clark and possemen too numerous to mention. It was a coalition born of convenience rather than the conviction that a revolutionary change in racial-economic roles was needed. The black poor—shunned by white poor, themselves utterly unorganized and needful of allies—were locked in a local version of the broader, nationwide struggle over the Poverty Program, a struggle waged between the poor on one hand and defenders of the status quo on the other.

Theoretically, the poor were guaranteed one-third representation on the boards of directors of Community Action Programs,[36] where ultimate decisions of policy, hiring, and fund allocation are made. This arbitrary fragmentation was designed to insure that the poor weren't shut out completely. The protection was largely illusory. People who had never had more than a tenuous control over their destinies were relegated to a minority one-third status in a noble experiment at destiny-making. They could suggest but not determine. They could denounce the status quo but not alter it. In a few isolated cases, where militant, experienced organizations of the poor already existed, political techniques could be employed to reduce, in small measure, the Poverty Program's built-in inequities. These inevitably were cases where black civil rights activity had been manifest. But poor whites, for all their pathetic self-delusions of racial grandeur, could not muster even these limited shows of assertion. They are psychologically shattered by society's insistence that failure is an individual sin, never a social crime, and this renders them politically inept, particularly in the South, where the behavioral bite bites deepest.[37] The overall result was that the habitually powerless Southern black entered the Poverty Program with his powerlessness certified by one-third representation and further diluted by internecine Negro strife; the poor white rarely entered at all.

Resultant antipoverty efforts found Selma without a Head Start program, since county and city school systems did not comply with Washington integration directives, and with only a handful of white and black young, and chronically unemployed adults, absorbed into OEO work programs. These were supplying city and county with the kind of free labor remindful of chain-gang days but doing little or nothing for the participants' long-range vocational needs. So many were employed at tasks like garbage pickup and sewage-ditch digging that the program was called Operation Draino.

As unsatisfactory as the poverty programs were, some whites deplored the minor equities they had provided Negroes. Moving down Main Street past the music shop flowerpots, a car passes the small storefront OEO office [38] beside the hundred-year-old Albert Hotel. The OEO office is a newcomer without distinctions; the Albert claims two: built largely by slaves, it is the only hotel in the United States patterned after the Doges Palace in Venice, and the only hotel where the late Dr. Martin Luther King, Jr., was punched in the face by a fanatic.[39] The next-door OEO office has a minor claim to fame. After black agitation forced the relocation of a Negro secretary from a back desk to a more visible front desk, Selma Mayor Joe Smitherman had the office padlocked. Mayor Smitherman had been a poor boy himself unable to graduate from high school, but the experience had not enriched his understanding of poverty, particularly where black people were concerned.

A few blocks beyond the office, across the railroad tracks and then right on Jeff Davis Avenue, the visitor taking the long way to Joe Johnson's place comes to the old Interlaken Cotton Gin, just down the road from Brown's Chapel, where the emotional fires of the Selma Movement burned brightest. The gin, Negro-owned for eighty years, houses the Southwest Alabama Farmers Co-operative Association, a target for such disparate figures as the late Alabama Governor Lurleen Wallace, the Reverend Reese, and Mayor Smitherman. The co-op began in 1966 and was incorporated in January, 1967, with perhaps seven hundred small Negro farmers from ten counties. Most were tenants, some were owners, all were finding it virtually impossible to go it alone. Boxed in on small farms that barely broke even, much less showed a profit,[40] they could not cut their costs by quantity purchase of seeds or fertilizer. Most still plowed behind mules. Marketing individually, they were at the mercy of roving buyers or local processers who could pay what they chose for the basic crops of cucumbers, okra, peas, beans, and potatoes. And they could not afford transportation costs to carry their produce to distant, better markets. The Extension Service roundly ignored them when it tested soil or disseminated insect-control information and the Farmers Home Administration skimped on the very kind of loans they needed if they ever were to advance.[41] Individually and as a group, they were headed the way of the Buck Simses and Charlie Whites, and it was clear that no one in the state of Alabama or the nation was going to help them unless they helped themselves.

The story of how SWAFCA was organized, the enormous difficulties in persuading black men so long dependent for their existence on white approval to risk white censure by uniting is a chronicle in itself. Stoutly respectable organizations like the Southern Regional Council gave important informational help. Individuals like Shirley Mesher, a free-lance civil rights activist, energetically assisted in planning and recruiting. She had come to Selma in 1965, an uncompromising woman with a militant personality that frequently grated on white and black "moderates," and had a traumatic effect on local segregationists. They called her a communist and worse, and she became a full-fledged issue when SWAFCA applied for a badly needed OEO grant of half a million dollars.

The late Governor Lurleen Wallace told Washington that the co-op had been formed to further a Black Panther political conspiracy.[42] Alabama Democratic Congressman William Nichols declared: "The leadership of the cooperative is insufficient to handle such a project. We felt along with other members of the Alabama delegation that if the project were to be funded the leadership should be strengthened to include directly members of the *State Extension Service and other agriculture officials.*" [43]

Co-op farmers wondered at the congressman's sudden concern for their welfare. Sheriff Wilson Baker also displayed hitherto undetectable interest in poor black farmers; Miss Mesher, he said, was the bone in the throat of Alabama approval and the way she was using the farmers was something awful. The Reverend Reese, his leadership increasingly opposed by Dallas County Negroes restive over slow progress, agreed. So, for a time, did Father Crowley, whose Roman Catholic St. Elizabeth Church in service to Negroes still is quaintly called a mission. But Father Crowley did some soul-searching and decided that Miss Mesher notwithstanding, the co-op would be good for all those bodies and souls spread over ten counties. He swung his support to SWAFCA.

While the application pended in Washington, state troopers at first harassed the few trucks the co-op had scrounged up. The owner of a pickling concern, accustomed to having Negro cucumber farmers over a barrel on prices, ruined a SWAFCA contract in Michigan by telling the buyer there that co-op cucumbers had been grown from seed stolen from him. The Michigan man heard SWAFCA's side of the story, said he was convinced by it, but pulled out of the deal because he didn't want the variety of trouble threatened by the pickler.

The concerted white Alabama effort to block poor people

from improving their lot was a sad reminder of the old story about the elderly Mississippi Negro trying to register who was called on to interpret the state constitution to qualify. No sooner had he interpreted one section than he was asked about another, until finally when the question came for the sixth time, "Now what does that mean, uncle?" the man replied: "I guess it means I can't vote."

In May, 1967, Sargent Shriver's Office of Economic Opportunity approved a $399,967 grant to the co-op and Governor Wallace promptly vetoed it. Shriver—who later left a faltering OEO to become American ambassador to France—could have just as promptly overridden the veto but he moved cautiously during a period when the Democratic Administration was trying to placate its segregationist elements for the sake of party unity.[44] But the case for SWAFCA was undeniable, and in July Shriver overrode the veto. The co-op, which had been charged with communism along with Black Pantherism, announced the good news in a mimeographed sheet bearing this note:

> Please share these messages in church and in other meetings. God blessed this community when it stood together in self-help. Let us continue to be blessed. Together. With God.

The grant had not yet taken effect when a visitor came by Interlaken Gin in midsummer. Under a tin shed in a dusty yard, which would be snowy with cotton fuzz in ginning season, okra trucked in from ten counties was being sorted on an old conveyor belt grader designed for potatoes. Negro sorters hired locally were making $1 to $1.25 an hour but experienced hands were in short supply; the supervisor was a one-armed white man from Orlando, Florida. But produce was said to be moving well at the Birmingham market, with cucumbers, for example, bringing one and a half cents more a pound than county dealers would pay. To farmers, pennies per pound mean dollars in profit and, with enough profit on enough crops during the season, the difference between defenseless indebtedness and a dollar or two to call their own. Fifteen or twenty families were pooling money to hire trucks to haul their produce to the gin until the grant—hopefully—could provide a truck for each county.

Calvin Osborne, gin owner, is a force of undetermined authority in SWAFCA, technically hired by its board of directors but actually indispensable since SWAFCA uses his physical plant to process cotton and other crops, and another plant would be hard to come by. He also supplies vital marketing expertise and self-assurance in dealing with white men. He inherited the gin from his father and runs a profitable farm on the side. Osborne, about forty, trim and neatly moustached, is every inch the antithesis of the struggling farmers dependent on him. In his air-conditioned office (one wall hung with an anomalous painting of an old-time gin with a young Negro arriving in a mule-drawn cart loaded with cotton while an old Negro with frizzly white hair sits smiling, cap in hand and pure darky, begging at the gin door) Osborne exudes commercial confidence.[45] It gleams from his diamond ring, his gold watch, his crisp straw hat.

"Our major problems now are farmer education and plant personnel," he says. "Farmers have to get reeducated to new methods and refinanced for land and equipment. To make a go around here—and I'm talking about just subsistence—you must have at least forty good acres with five of cotton allotment for ready cash and the rest in okry, soybeans, maybe cabbage, which has a big potential, etc. The FHA hasn't been doing its job on loans for land and machinery. They have to loosen up on collateral and credit requirements for a farmer like Joe Johnson, our chairman. He's farming with nothing, working hard for nothing. This year he won't even make nothing the way his crops have gotten ahead of him while he runs around for the co-op. But in the future with co-op earnings, maybe somebody like him can build up a credit balance, get some equipment and acreage, start to farm in the twentieth century.

"The way it works, co-op members get spot cash when they bring in produce and a straight count they can trust. At the end of the year, any dividends we have from sales will be divided as profit. We want to set up grading substations in each county. We want to buy tractors that members can rotate around, get out from behind the mule. It's a tremendous job and the grant—except for purchasing trucks and expenses around here—will only cover a small part.

"But we expect to double membership next year as word gets around that SWAFCA really delivers to the small farmer. And that it's a farmers' co-op, not Black Power or civil rights. Now I don't mean to run you off but this is a busy time."

One nagging question. In the fall, when cotton starts pouring in for ginning, how can he handle both it and the co-op vegetable harvest?

Osborne allowed himself a smile.

"We're gonna gin cotton at Interlaken," he says, "and blow cotton dust all over the vegetable graders. And they're gonna keep grading."

Maybe the co-op will make it and maybe it won't. It had doubled membership by mid-1968, and a vital $800,000 loan was finally approved by the FHA after another epic struggle between the SWAFCA and officials in Alabama and Washington. (Alabama FHA Director Robert Bamberg later testifies before the USCRA that Negro farmers' complaints that they can't get adequate FHA loans "goes back to this. In many cases, our nigger population has small acreage.") SWAFCA must depend on continued government backing during the early, critical stages. Joe Johnson and friends have a long row to hoe. It's only fifteen minutes from Interlaken gin out to his place. First you drive the River Road asphalt for a few miles, then left onto a firm, graded dirt farm road running by the houses of some white farmers, then left again onto a decaying dirt road [46] that eventually dissolves into two tire tracks running parallel to a hump of dried grass between fields of high corn that hem in the car as it bumps and slows and searches out potholes until finally it breaks clear of the corn onto a path bordering a pea patch, and ahead, by a shack like a thousand others, there is a shady chinaberry tree where, at Joe Johnson's place, the road ends. But it may begin there, too.

8

The Only Light Is the Co-op

FIRST: the house and yard. The air smells of sunlight on grass. Small country sounds and large country silences. Chickens scratch by the shack wall weathered an oyster gray. A white duck scoops water from a hollowed-out log trough, throws its head back, and gargles the water down. Under the chinaberry, a red-wattled turkey with suspicious eyes gabbles, observing. In the swept dirt in front of the empty porch, a car tire has been cut and peeled back like a radish to hold flowers; fat bees move among them and dragonflies hover, slivers of emerald levitated and glistening. The eye wonders why the shack seems strangely unencumbered, then realizes there are no electrical or telephone lines running into it. There *is* a wire washline stretched between a log pole and a barren mulberry tree. Patched clothes and sheets made of flour sacks sewn together are drying, and a notched sapling props the line in the middle where it droops. There is a water pump near the mulberry and beyond it a hand plow leaning against a corncrib sagging in four different directions and farther beyond in a field two mules are grazing tranquilly. There is no clue to time. It might be 1930, 1920. Except for the peeled car tire, it might even be a drowsy July afternoon in the 1800's.

At first there is no hint of time in the cornfield either. Two dark figures in the distance, a man and a gangling boy, are walking through rows of stunted plants. Grass, in some places, is growing as high as the corn, rustling on a breeze that suddenly carries the high-powered drone from a far-off car and brings the day up to date. Joe Johnson and his son Willie are throwing down white beads of chemical fertilizer; they wave hello and stop to talk at the end of the row. The father is in khakis, plaid shirt, and porkpie hat, a man about fifty, weary-eyed, sinewy, deliberate in speech and movement. Willie, in Levis, a loose sweatshirt, and a mask of oversized sunglasses, is mannerly but cool, a listener to the conversation, somehow urbane, squatting at the edge of the cornfield and suggesting cynicism in his silent posture.

"First I learned of the co-op idea was through the Southern Christian Leadership Conference," Joe Johnson says, rolling a cigarette from a can of Prince Albert crimp cut. "They came through gettin' people redished to vote an' we heard about an okry co-op in Mississippi where black farmers went on to buy combines an' corn pullers an' sold for a good rate. You see, the average Negro—an' that means the majority—do not get any help from the ASC [Agricultural Stabilization and Conservation Service].[47]

"There isn't a Negro on the Dallas County ASC an' never has been though they say there's an alternate now. The way it works is, communities elect committeemen an' they vote for the three regulars an' two alternates on the county committee. That's where all the power to give allotments is, on the county committee. An' it makes up the community committee ballots. I ran in the last election an' had good support. But you know the people in the ASC office, they crooked it up. They only put five white names on the ticket but ten or twelve colored names to confuse folks an' split the vote.[48]

"We knew we had to do somethin'. Southern Regional an' a lot of other people gave us good encouragement. First, we had to get a board of directors for the co-op, two men from each county, an' they had to pick a chairman of the board who would be president. It took a lot of doin', people weren't used to that sort of thing. The chairman was offered to several an' they refused. Then someone put me up an' I didn't refuse. In April, a bunch of us loaded up in two cars an' went to Washington to see what was holdin' up the OEO grant." [49]

Answering questions, Johnson sketched the life history that led him, at an age when a hard-working man might think of easing off or retiring, to a house without electricity, a farm without a tractor, an existence with no more root than one of the cornstalks behind him. The broad, black strokes of the outline were a familiar Southern story; the details particular to Joe Johnson. He was born to a tenant family of nine children, his father doing well with enough hands at home to farm seventy acres of cotton back before the Depression, his mother a woman "pretty determined about education." So Johnson went through the ninth grade before his father died and the sons had to leave school to work the farm. His own farming life began with decent prospects after he married and tenanted on one hundred and fifty acres owned by a Negro in the late thirties. But the spread was sold to a white man.

"I'd style him a slave owner," Johnson said. "He wanted to tell you what to plant, when to plant, how to plant. He wanted halves, but at the end of the year it turned out to be whole. Couldn't stand that so I left."

There were years of ups and downs, the years measured out in bales of cotton, the margin between want and having slim as the few pennies' fluctuation in the price of a pound of cotton. How much cash did he ever wind up with in the very best farming year of his life after debts were paid? Eight hundred dollars? Seven hundred? Six? Five? [50]

"Five hundred?" he says and laughs. "Oh, my Lord, if I had ever made five hundred dollars I'd be boasting it pretty high. Like my woman says, I can't tell the difference from the end of the year to the beginning as far as cash money goes. An' they keep squeezin' you down more every year until now I don't got but only a four-acre allotment with two and a half planted. This land here wasn't really taken care of before an' you got to fertilize it real high. That costs money so I went to FHA for an operation loan. But they said they'd run out of money.*

* New York *Times*, March 15, 1967: "PENTAGON TRIPLES SPENDING ON DEFOLIATION IN VIETNAM—The United States has tripled crop destruction and defoliation of jungles in Vietcong areas of Vietnam, according to indications from the Pentagon." The story explained that the Defense Department first spent $10 million a year on defoliants and herbicides, increased it to $32 million and planned to spend $53 million if the war continued. There may not be a direct, provable relation between FHA's inability to lend Joe Johnson money to grow crops and Defense Department spending to kill them. But there is a suggestion that national priorities—to say nothing of morality—may be distorted.

"Rent here is a hundred and fifty dollars a year an' that's one bale out of a little over two I'll make. The owner won't even put in light lines. This was the first time since we been married we didn't have light. Kerosene lamps, that's what we have. The fact is you can't get no decent cooperation from these people nohow. When the co-op got goin' good, I asked the county agent to give soil tests like he does the whites. He made two promises he'd be out in this field an' he ain't arrived yet." [51]

Compressed together, the facts of Johnson's life seem to form a massive complaint, a drawn-out whine. But this is a distortion of reportage; it is not Johnson's style. Like most farmers, accustomed to waiting on seasons and making lonely judgments about the soil, the elements, his capacities, Johnson is patient, dry in speech, cautious. Still, being a black farmer in the South builds a store of knowledge never found in a white farmer's almanac, and it is mostly negative—for example, white cotton buyers paying a long staple price when a Negro brings in short staple cotton; a friend of Johnson's with an exceptionally large black allotment making twenty-five bales in 1966 but being evicted in 1967 when he refused to sign over acreage diversion checks to the landowner. Johnson guaranteed his own unpopularity among whites even before the co-op by insisting that he cash his diversion checks (last year $150) and gin his cotton under *his* name, not the owner's.

"Put the white man's name on top of the ticket," he says, "an' he gets the money from the gin an' gives the Negro what he wants to. Far as diversion checks go, any time my land is put by an' I don't get the check, I'll stop farmin'."

Despite the complex of reasons for a man's being poor, failure at fifty raises its own pernicious questions about how a man has handled his role of family provider. Johnson says that his wife is probably back from visiting a neighbor if anyone would like to talk to her. He and Willie, who has coolly absorbed all the talk, go off down another row.

Mrs. Johnson, mother of seven, is sitting on the porch, leaning over a big galvanized washbucket, cutting up baby peaches that float in a fragrant wash of peelings. She's about fifty, very dark against a white cotton dress with faded floral print and wide sleeves that accentuate the spidery movements of her slender arms. Her body is so spare it seems to have been flayed down by the years to an irreducible essence, tough and supple and womanly in a way that has nothing to do with full-hipped roundness or amplitude of breasts. Her long and liquid brown fingers plash into the sweet water and rise with languid discipline to pare a peach. Her face with young bones and old eyes is grave and remote, a beautiful African look.

"You'll excuse me," she says. "White folks make me nervous. I just don't get out amongst them lest I get scared a lot."

But she is persuaded to talk about her seven children. Five have already gone through high school and are in the North, one in Chicago and the others in New York City. Still at home are Willie, in the ninth grade, and Frederick, passing to the fifth. The son in Chicago works in a factory; Joe Jr. in Brooklyn is with a moving company; Dorothy in Queens, a shorthand secretary; her sister Ivory in Harlem, married to a Vietnam veteran. Butler, eighteen, went up earlier in the summer to stay with the girl in Queens and look for work. It is a family record of migrant stability remarkable in a time of its opposites [52] and suggests that if Johnson's fortunes have gone down, a sense of values remains intact.

"I sure is glad they left," Mrs. Johnson says. "They couldn't get any kind of good job here. Joe Jr. finished high school an' he just walked an' walked an' walked day after day up an' down these roads lookin' for work. These white folks won't give 'em nothin'. I don't care how much learnin' a Negro got. All he can do is get a job in white folks' house cleanin'. They so mean here the post office made me pay five cents 'cause my daughter left off the zone number on the envelope when she wrote. My children's been askin' me to go up there but I ain't willin'." Her voice is a soft monotone, at times detached as if the story she told were about someone else. But at the question, Why won't you go north? Mrs. Johnson smiles and her tone is animated. "It just looks like I love the country."

And if Willie and Frederick followed the pattern and left home eventually?

"If all the kids left, I reckon I'd go to the home an' get me one. I wrote my married daughter an' told her if she wanted to go to work to send her baby down. I'd surely love to care for her."

Nowhere in the tables of black migration north is there a column measuring the loss to a mother of her children and grandchildren. And nowhere in any table or study is there a measure of what it takes in a woman to see five children through high school under the conditions of Negro tenant life, and at fifty to be seeing two more through in a shack with no refrigerator, no light, no bathroom, no phone.

"Joe, my old man, he's steady, he always tried as best he could," Mrs. Johnson says. "But it's pretty tough, pretty tough. I'm still washin' on the rub-board an' when you got three men you got somethin'. Then with food—it be's a scuffle. Sometimes it's just how much I can scull up here an' there. Tonight we gonna have some peas in whitemeat an' a peach pie from these a neighbor gave."

Mrs. Johnson wipes her fingers, slick with the sweet of the peaches, and goes inside to fire the woodstove to make the pie and put up the remaining peaches. The house, like all shacks, exhales a burned smell from the fireplace and stove; the walls and ceiling are smoke-stained. The ceiling is reinforced by cardboard cartons, one international patch stamped MADE IN AUSTRIA. Other patches come from pages of *Ebony* magazine. The rough plank floors are swept as clean as a barracks before inspection and on a tightly made bed an Army sergeant might admire there is a decorative display: a toy bear wrapped in plastic and a framed magazine photo of John F. Kennedy.

"Do the children resent us for their poor lives?" she says to a question. "How do you mean? Oh, hold it against us? Lord, no. They understand. Yes, they understand. They do feel like me it's the fault of the white people. That's the truth. I know we ain't gettin' no fair deal an' my children know it. What they was givin' you for your work was so little it didn't pay an' then they stopped givin' you that."

She pokes sticks into a stove of gleaming white metal, its stylish appearance incongruous with the primitive fuel. Mrs. Johnson's hands holding the sticks lose the liquid grace of the peach cutting, turn rough to the task, jamming down the wood, snapping it. The scene suddenly is quaint, evocative of a simpler past that rouses nostalgia in a visitor who has never actually known it. The piny smoke curling up from the sticks, the sweet peaches waiting to be jarred, how amiable it all is. How amiable until the visitor pictures his own mother barefoot under a roof of MADE IN AUSTRIA cartons patched with *Ebony,* dining on fatback and peas, heating water for dishes after years of childbearing, child-raising, and massaging the old washboard, day after week, after month, after year.

The Johnson boys and their father have come onto the porch, Frederick materializing from somewhere. His mother calls him.

"Ma'am?" he calls back in that soft-voiced tone of respect that falls as a Southern blessing, black and white, on Northern parental ears.

Frederick is told to show his schoolbooks and lessons. His handwriting on a fourth-grade history test is clear and neat; one question answered correctly is how many years has it been since Lincoln freed the slaves; his score is 98 percent. There is English homework.

"Why couldn't you ride on a butterfly?"

"Who makes more noise walking, you or a cat?"

"Which can fly farther, a chicken or a crow?"

His answers all are correct but the questions scarcely challenge him; his eyes smile at the joke in asking such questions. Until three years before, the one store selling schoolbooks had a pile for whites and a separate one for Negroes with "easier" books, You paid your money and you got their choice. The Civil Rights Commission report tells that in 1950 36 percent of Southern rural white youth had a high school education or better compared with 11 percent black. The difference was 25 percent. Ten years later, 48 percent of white and 23 percent of black had gone through high school, the difference still 25 percent. And this was for rural families off the farm. Quantitatively all the percentages are lower for farm children, and qualitatively the education of a black child like Frederick Johnson in the fourth grade raises the question of riding a butterfly.

"I can see things startin' to tighten up more here due to the co-op an' votin'," Johnson says. "But they'll never force it back to the old days. Under no circumstances. Old or young, a man won't collapse back to that."

"These young Negroes you see here ain't gonna go back into slavery," Mrs. Johnson says, making a sudden entrance onto the porch. "They know how they been done. There wasn't never a county agent in their lives come out to see them or me. They know. They fight till they die."

"You see," continues her husband, "before, the biggest, the onliest hope a Negro farmer had was cotton. He didn't have enough land for cattle, enough money to buy stock, an' cotton produced better cash to the acre than anything else.[53] Still does if you could get the acres. With the trend changin' to vegetable farmin' the future can be more brighter. But you gotta have machines an' markets an enough land so that a crop like okry—bringin' less than half an acre than cotton—will pay.

"That's where the co-op comes in.[54] It can hold corn off the harvest market to get a better price. Same with cotton. Holdin' off might mean ten or fifteen dollars more a bale. With okry, cukes, an' peas the co-op can find you a better market. We hope it's gonna mean gettin' tractors so I can say good-bye to those mules. We can chop down on prices all along the line buyin' an' maybe see some way ahead. That's why they want to wreck it.

"Once we started up, I tried to buy three hundred tons at the Centrilla Fertilizer Factory an' they wouldn't sell to us. We finally bought in Atlanta at a good discount. But at the same time, you see, some local white businesses are comin' aroun'. Some of the compresses are comin' to us now to get our cotton crop. So we're makin' progress. One thing you can bet: if it wasn't for SWAFCA, hundreds of Alabama black farmers wouldn't be farmin' at all this year. Whether they'll be farmin' next year depends on how good we survive."

Johnson does not go into why whites want to wreck SWAFCA. It is at once ancient knowledge not worth explaining, and at the same time beyond understanding. Mrs. Johnson reverts for a moment to an old vision, which once was the only vision, as she says good-bye.

"God, that's my all in all," she says. "He helps me. All what's come to me has come through the Good Lord. If it wasn't for

Him I don't think I could possibly make it. Bad as it gets I just say, that's the way He have me to go, I reckon."

But Joe Johnson, who works hard and drinks only an occasional beer, who has spent his scant portion on educating his children, who risks eviction by leading that which is the serpentine body of the anti-Christ to many white Alabamians, Joe Johnson has caught a new vision and will not let it go.

"The only source of light is the co-op," he says. "Build a strong co-op an' things can change. Let it go an'—"

The hand-rolled Prince Albert cigarette hangs on his outthrust lower lip. The unspoken is obvious. Johnson is a tired man who knows the odds. In this way he is like most Southern farm Negroes dwelling in poverty that ranges from amiable to unbearable. But he sees a road out from his place and he believes, despite his history, that he is on his way.

9

The Beautiful Blond Children of Bainbridge

"I'M ready for the asylum," says Mrs. Lottie Fergurson. "You'd get thirty-five dollars for turning me in."

But she says it with a smile at the beautiful blond children swarming around her on the unpainted shack porch on the main road into Bainbridge, Decatur County, Georgia. There is no water in the shack and none in the backyard either; the children tote it from a well across the highway. But the family looks clean, their worn clothes scrubbed and pressed, blond hair shining. There are seven children at home now, and keeping them in shape, even keeping count, is why Mrs. Fergurson sometimes thinks the asylum is beckoning.

"There's one twelve," she says, shaking her head at a small boy who wanders out of the shack with a giant cornflakes box a third as big as himself. "Next nine, eight, seven, six, an' two. How many do that make? Seven? Oh no, the girl fourteen. Sally's layin' down inside with the sunburn. She's the one quit high school this year 'cause she didn't have the things the other girls did an' her daddy didn't make her go. I just tell you, it takes clothes an' all to keep a family this size goin'. Diapers, Lord! When one has shoes the others don't. If it weren't for the Salvation Army, they wouldn't have that."

Mrs. Fergurson's husband is at work in the local crate factory where—after fifteen years—he makes about $55 a week before deductions as a machine operator at $1.40 an hour. His

71

story is not new among poor Southern white men; it is very old.

"He hasn't got no education," his wife explains. "He can't even write his name. It's hard on him 'cause he can't write. He come from a poor family an' his daddy made him work in the fields so he never could go to school. I went to the eighth myself. But when you start out with nothin' like him, you have to take what you can get." [55]

Mrs. Fergurson's manner is apologetic. She looks around her and appears to see the familiars of her proverty through the eyes of a stranger seeing them for the first time. She is forty-two years old and has borne ten children. Two older girls are married and an eighteen-year-old boy who dropped out of high school is away, trying to make it on his own. Her face is showing the wizened marks of white women who grow old and tired before their time; but her eyes are alert and friendly, she wears bright lipstick, and her fine auburn hair hangs down at schoolgirl length. Obviously, it is her pride.

"We never heard anythin' about government food here," she says. "We make food off twenty dollars a week. The house don't cost but six dollars a month. But light runs eight, the gas six an' the rest just goes on old bills. We eat a lot of peas, smoked bake ends, and whitemeat. We'll have one of them chickens sometimes. But I can't buy no milk, no, sir. You can't at fifty-four cents a half gallon. The five in school get a free lunch—the oldest boy pays it back some by cleanin' up the school kitchen an' bathroom.

"But lots of folks aroun' here have troubles, not just us. The only work is at the factory an' they got a union but what the union does I don't know.[56] 'Cept take the dues. My man was out sick last winter an' I thought if you took sick they was supposed to help your family. The union didn't give us enough to buy a twenty-five pound sack of flour. An' that's the truth. An' when you're a workin' man here, the family can't get no welfare.

"He don't have no insurance so we pay the doctor a little at a time. He's been real good about it. But I can tell you the hospital won't take you without a deposit unlest you're dyin'. They used to have a free county clinic for the children but it went out of business an' they put an old folks home in there.

With one thing an' another, you never catch up. I never have gone out to work an' that might've helped some. But I just had one after another."

The children have all been healthy, although there is no agency that checks their health. (It is an American anomaly that various levels of government inspect automobiles, restaurant kitchens, meat-packing houses, and tax returns, but leave the living conditions of the poor and the health of their children to chance.)

There are four rooms in the Fergurson shack, crowded with beds and children's clothing piled and hung everywhere; but the house is neat, the floor scoured clean. The kitchen in midday is so dark that a white gas range gives off a luminescent gleam; like Mrs. Fergurson's hair, it is the family pride, chipping out $5 each month from Mr. Fergurson's paycheck. Placed strategically around it on the floor are tin cans to catch early morning rain leaking from the roof. Outside on the rear porch, a line of tin buckets and gasoline cans are filled with water from the well across the highway. The rambling backyard is cluttered with wrecked cars, tireless, rusting, sides caved in and windshields shattered, as if a pileup had occurred in a stock car race and the drivers climbed out and left, and no one ever called the wreckers to clear the track. Mrs. Fergurson explains that her husband bought them over the years to sell spare parts and never has gotten around to having them hauled away. Poverty breeds its own diseases, and inertia is endemic.

The barefoot children are playing around the gaunt remains of a towering dead cypress, lightning-shattered and stripped of its bark, the wood bleached bone-white over the years. There are cases of soft-drink bottles lying near the base in a welter of rubble where skinny chickens scratch; it is a setting ready for a touring company of *Tobacco Road* players. But the children, by their artless presence, suggest a different tale, not of depravity realized but of innocence and beauty making the most of their brief time of grace. There is Dorothy Anne, seven, with old-fashioned tumbling curls and a smile that makes you blink; Donald, six, who lifts the cornflakes box and is wolfing them down by the fistful, laughing at what a heller he is; there is

Betty, nine, whose blond hair hangs straighter than her sister's and whose smile is slow and secret.

The children are slowly learning what they are and what they are likely to become. The oldest girl, who quit high school because she lacks things other girls have, never presents herself while the visitor is questioning her mother. Raymond, twelve, listens moodily as Mrs. Fergurson explains that her children play pretty much among themselves.

"There's another family right down the road with children," she says. "But they're high class an' don't associate with poor people."

The younger ones have gained clues to their ultimate identities by going to the Salvation Army and the First Baptist Church to try on secondhand clothing. At Christmas, the Veterans of Foreign Wars bring presents. Their mother keeps them respectably clean and sees that they don't go hungry. But she states as an unalterable fact that there is no way her children can go to high school; she knows that there isn't any way the spare financial resources of the family can ever fatten; she sees the proof in her life of what that can mean. Mrs. Fergurson is also aware that accident, illness, or a layoff could erase the present hairline margin between family decency and disintegration. A visitor to the Fergurson shack wonders: if something ugly lies in wait for these beautiful children, what lies in wait for a country that will permit ugliness to ambush them?

10

Bad Baker

BAKER, just over the line from Decatur, is one of the twenty-three counties of southwest Georgia. They comprise a mostly ragged crazy quilt of political enclaves with populations about half black, half white, including some of the poorest in the nation.[57] While the area is overwhelmingly rural, farming is a diminishing source of revenue and by the year 2000 (assuming there is a southwest Georgia then) the Agriculture Department estimates that farm employment will be half what it is today. The section is in urgent need of area redevelopment and county consolidation that could pool resources, revenues, and planning. But politicians holding on grimly to their lean fiefs will not move in the humane and logical direction of cooperation and visionary planning that transcends county lines.

Bad Baker used to be pronounced as one word by Negroes, as Damnyankee once was, and occasionally still may be, by white Southerners. Law enforcement was on a pathological level, and during the early days of the Movement for an activist (or even a reporter) to enter Bad Baker was akin to a Christian dropping into the lion pit of the Roman Coliseum. Today, Baker has changed for the better, with more responsible men (still all white) running the county; but things in general remain bad. On the sad roster of America's three hundred poorest counties, Baker stands thirty-seventh. It is the only county in Georgia, residents say, without a doctor. There is a small garment factory in the county seat of Newton that employs a handful of white women; the only town jobs for black women are domestic work at $10 to $15 a week. Four plantations in the county devoted to pine, quail, and cotton cover 45 percent of Baker's land.[58] Black tractor drivers on the plantations recently won $1-an-hour minimum salaries. The corporations owning the vast acreage immediately began charging rent on most houses which hitherto had been "free" for the driver-occupants making $35 and $40 for a 60-hour week.

More than half of Baker's 4,500 inhabitants receive the free federal commodity food. The food distribution program is run by the antipoverty Community Action Council and paid for entirely by the Office of Economic Opportunity. On a recent day, across the street from the town hall once synonymous with the worst racial repression east of the Alabama line, white and Negro families came to get their monthly allotment. The food was being handed out by white and Negro women in fresh white uniforms under the direction of a white male official. Recipients in Baker and other counties participating in the commodity program are usually certified by the local welfare departments. Always allowing for abuses by individual officials, most anyone in the county who needs commodities gets them. Whether they get enough is something else. The Agriculture Department says, "These programs are not intended to provide a complete diet, only to supplement the participant's food supply." It does not say what happens when a family can't buy the milk, vegetables, fruit, and occasional meat and fish that the commodities are supposed to be supplementing. A Negro mother picking up for a family of six takes away:

3 2-lb. packages of dry beans
5 5-lb. sacks of cornmeal
4 1-lb. packages of flour
4 2-lb. packages of rice
4 4½-lb. packages of dried milk
4 3-lb. tins of lard
2 3-lb. packages of rolled wheat
6 2-lb. cans of tinned beef
5 2-lb. packages of grits
3 1-lb. packages of raisins

The supplement insures that no one will presently starve in Baker.[59]

Many recipients are the families of day laborers, farm hands, tractor drivers, or whatever name is applied to the growing ranks of black men in Baker County (and throughout the South) who can no longer make it on their own land or by tenant farming. A race of hired hands inside the Negro race seems to be evolving.[60] Some of the reasons for this have been encountered on earlier pages; the Negroes involved often use the word "squeeze" to sum up the various pressures, ranging from land inadequate to begin with to denial of federal services. Whether or not this is part of a white ideological conspiracy to make blacks either migrate or become helots is a fine point for debate. But some facts are suggestive. In Mississippi, for example, a hard core of 26,000 Negro tractor drivers has come into existence, men who do no farming on their own but tend white men's cotton in the Delta at $6 or $7 a day (possibly going higher with new $1-an-hour minimum wage laws applicable to certain farms). While this core was forming, in five years' time between 1954 and 1959, the number of Delta tenant farmers dropped 60 percent, from 83,000 to 33,000; concurrently, the number of hired workers (mostly black, as were the tenants) rose 62 percent, from 24,000 to 39,000. The final figure in this grouping shows that 60,000 Negroes between the ages of fifteen and forty-four left the state between 1960 and 1965.[61] An important factor in these shifts, aside from any conspiratorial racial "squeeze," was technological advances in cotton farming that made it more profitable for landowners to hire hands to work their land instead of leasing it to tenants. So no precise correlation between statistics and the "squeeze" theory can be made. But the bold pattern remains clear in Mississippi and elsewhere in the Black Belt: black farmers eliminated, black migrants dispatched, black hired hands available on call.

In Georgia, the purely racist overtones in this pattern, apart from technological expedients, prompted an unusual action in 1967. The number of Negro farmers in the state had plummeted from 50,000 in 1950 to 11,000.[62] The Georgia Advisory Commission to the U.S. Civil Rights Commission asked the Agriculture Department to cut all federal money from the state's Extension Service (one-third of a $2.7 million expenditure) until Georgia stopped discrimination against Negroes in farm programs.

"Negroes in Georgia believe they are being phased out as farmers," Secretary Freeman was told. "To the day they retire or die, Negro farmers in Georgia are relegated to the status of second-class citizens."

This was the first time such a demand had been made in the history of the federal Extension Service and nobody really expected anything to come of it. So far, nothing has. To two black men sitting on a shack porch ten minutes' drive from the Newton commodity center, the protest—had they heard of it— would have seemed academic. They are products of the system of natural and man-made attrition that is reducing many rural Negro men to a race of hired hands. Beale says that hired farm workers "are being drawn from an increasingly atypical section of society . . . hiring those who from poor education, lack of vocational training or other limitations cannot succeed as farmers or do better in nonagricultural jobs." [63] Clinical truth by its nature omits human essence. Here are two men, one young, the other old, at least a generation apart, but their histories run a disturbing parallel.

At fifty, Ben Lee has committed poverty's dual sin of getting old and getting sick. Not that fifty is truly old. But he looks old and sounds older. He has been a sharecropper, a tenant, and finally a tractor driver. He remembers once in his farming life coming out of a year with $250 cash. Once. An auto wreck last October left him partially crippled and unable to work. Joe Chester, twenty-four, sitting next to him, was in the same wreck. He's still recovering from his injuries but able to work as a tractor driver on the Ischaway Plantation at $1 an hour. Lee has a son in the Army, an invalid wife, and two children at home—and a dour outlook.

"How do we make ends meet?" he says, repeating a question. "They don't hardly meet. I lived in this house all the years I was workin' for the Man tenant an' hand. He never said nothin' about puttin' us off now that I can't work. So I don't say nothin' to him so long as he don't say nothin' to me."

And life goes predictably on until tomorrow. Lee waves an indifferent invitation to inspect the shack. It is standard: clean, claustrophobic, depressing. Except for one bedroom wall from which the word STOKELY leaps out in foot-high letters. But it is not a den of Black Power. Lee has patched the wall with a poster advertising Stokely Bartlett Pears.

On the porch, Chester says that a wife, a four-year-old son, twins aged three, and a five-month-old baby are back on the Ischaway Plantation, dependent on the $45 a week he earns in season driving. Where Lee is heavy-headed, gruff, and somber of eye, Chester is shy, almost servile, with a quick, sweet smile showing dimples, and a soft voice. What was Lee like at twenty-four? What will Chester be like at fifty?

"Everytime I think about breaking out," Chester says, "I think about the kids. I just can't walk off an' leave 'em, suh. The way it is, I don't see no way for me to go to school again. I had the second grade before I went to work, but I can't read or write, no, suh."

"Fact is," Lee growls, "I stayed on the farm until I couldn't do nothin' else. Well, what could I do with no schoolin'? My daddy was on shares so we had to work with him."

"Now the baby, she don't get milk every day like she should," Chester says. "I work steady but when I'm workin' I can't get the commodities. Then, you see, I'm still payin' the hospital for the accident. It was one hundred and eighty-six dollars an' they take out each week. It don't leave much, no, suh."

"In debt all the time," says Lee, shifting his legs with a grunt. "Bein' black you're under a squeeze all the time. I had to depend on the Man for to pay my doctor bills previous. Now I don't know who would. If welfare didn't give me fifty dollars a month for the accident we couldn't do nothin'."

"No, suh," says Chester, "the kids ain't got the clothes they need. But I do the best I can. Suh? No, it don't worry me none that they'll have to do like me. 'Cause I reckon when they get big they'll raise up an' go out of here, not stick like their daddy."

"The problem is tough," says Lee. "All the civil rights hasn't made a speck of difference. Winter'll be comin' soon an' nothin' to buy wood with. In this old house the wind just about blows the chill off you. . . ."

Chester smiles, Lee glowers, but they get along easily together on the porch, sharing a common bond. They have been in the same wreck.

11

"Jo-Jo Is a Monkey"

AS bad as things still are in Baker, there is no natural law that says they must remain that way. The county—except for those ducal preserves of pine and quail—is poor, but the nation is rich. The county is so poor that the announcement board in a Negro church visited during the summer of 1967 listed the previous Sunday's attendance at seventy-two and the total donation as $2.49. The country is so rich that it can budget nearly $2 billion a year on a Poverty Program, a sum so staggering that it exceeds, for example, the Gross National Product of every country in Latin America except Chile. Still, the Poverty Program fails in Baker and everywhere. The failure might be taken as proof that it is fruitless to try to help American poor in any significant way. But what it actually proves is the futility of trying to help the poor with a relatively insignificant monetary and moral commitment. And even in poor little Baker, there is a tantalizing glimpse of the thrilling things that a true commitment could realize.

Like the church congregation scraping up $2.49 of a Sunday, the federal government is contributing nickels and dimes to Baker through the OEO, but without the churchgoers' excuse of empty pockets. The fact that the county even *has* a working Poverty Program is largely traceable to the civil rights activism there over the years; other dirt-poor counties in Georgia and elsewhere are not so fortunate because the underprivileged do not know how to organize to demand action by local officials.

The federal government legally cannot initiate those actions. So the national logic dictates that the most bereft areas receive the least assistance.

Baker has a Community Action Program with committee members divided evenly between whites and Negroes. Top-echelon direction is white, but this is not the tragic flaw, despite inequities that proceed from it. The tragic flaw is an incentive-crippling maze of bureaucratic channels combined with a criminal insufficiency of funding. Baker is one of four counties under the supervision of the Southwest Georgia OEO Council, with headquarters in Moultrie. In 1966, Baker had only a Head Start Center. People wanted, in addition, a Day Care Center in 1967, which would not only provide for children whose mothers worked (Negroes as domestics, whites in the garment factory) but would also create a few jobs. The Moultrie office said Baker could not have both but, according to Baker OEO officials, promised Day Care if Head Start were dropped. So Head Start was voted out in favor of Day Care, and today Baker County has neither.

"After we did what they asked," says CAP official Cecil Mulliford, "they came back and said they didn't have the money."

Mulliford is a tall, rather mournful white man of modest means who gives the impression that he is sincerely struggling to adapt old racial values to demands made by a new time. Many Negroes feel this struggle is not successful and that, successful on Mulliford's terms or not, it is not relevant to the need of black poor to control their immediate destiny.

"I know some Negroes aren't happy about what happened," Mulliford says. "But we didn't want it either. The people in Moultrie keep talking about Baker making 'in-kind' contributions if we want programs. We're a hundred percent poverty-stricken here, mister, an' we just can't get anything from the county commissioners. We thought we'd done a good job on drawing up a Day Care Center program. But Moultrie was changing it before we even got it submitted and then they threw it out altogether. Why can't somebody make them people let little poor counties alone?"

Despite bureaucratic frustrations, Baker wound up with something. It is called the Technical Rural Agricultural Program (TRAP) and behind the forbidding title is a humane concept, some practical value and—above all—the opportunity to bring personal dignity and self-esteem into lives that have rarely known them. TRAP qualifications are simple and sensible: applicants must be heads of households with a sixth-grade education or less, and making under $2,000 a year. For six months, they receive some kind of job training, their educations are begun or renewed, and some money—about $30 a week—goes into their pockets. If "six months" read "two or three years," one might feel confident that Washington legislators were seriously trying to salvage their fellow citizens when they designed the program; but in a climate of indifference the smallest shower of concern is welcome.

Baker's TRAP has all sorts of insurance for ultimate failure built into it.[64] While hundreds of whites and blacks needed it, there was originally money for only forty-eight places, and then it was discovered that this even was ten too many, so ten who had already signed up were lopped off before they started. One dropped out and then there were thirty-seven, thirteen men and twenty-four women, with Negroes in a slight majority but proportionately underrepresented. The youngest was nineteen, the oldest sixty-four. The women were to be taught sewing, the men carpentry and rudimentary plumbing. Making the unwarranted assumption that sufficient progress could be made by training a few hours a day to gain a job skill in six months, there was no provision for placement. The Newton garment factory, for example, is a small operation that employs no Negroes. Mrs. Bizzie Williams, a Negro who holds a BS and is a TRAP teacher at $50 a week, says:

"I put in an application there for myself before our program started. The owner said he'd let me know in two weeks. That was August, 1966, and I'm still waiting."

Mrs. R. I. Hudson, a white woman on the TRAP office staff, looks unhappy and resigned as she explains:

"We're just poor here, that's all. The mill is about the only employer and we hope it will cooperate when the people get trained but we just don't know. We're teaching them to fill out job applications anyway."

The Reverend James Johnson, a big, solidly built and self-assured Negro minister in overalls, chews a big cigar as he instructs his TRAP students in his trade of carpentry. The class is theoretically integrated, although the whites and blacks—all of them forty or older—make separate clusters as the Reverend Johnson shows them how to build a kitchen cabinet. He lights up the cigar and takes a calming puff as someone brings him a saw when he calls out for a T square. He does not try to kid himself or anyone else.

"The onliest thing in this program is to give a desire," he says. "We don't pretend to finish 'em up. They get a dollar an hour for six hours a day divided between here and the classroom. Plus forty cents for each dependent child up to four. You got ten you still get a dollar sixty. It's a help, that's all. But construction firms from out of the county that do jobs in Baker say they'll be glad to hire if the men show any ability. So there's a hope."

There is a hope. Slim as the wood shaving curling from the plane of George Dawkins, a fifty-eight-year-old Negro farmer who once had a few years of schooling long ago.

"It's helpin'," he says. "I think it is. In the school now, I couldn't even read before. But today I can pick up a letter an' if I go over it a few times I can understand it."

Sam Calhoun, sixty-one and white, was Baker County courthouse custodian for many years. The job carried no pension. He's sick with diabetes and looks it, and hasn't been able to work for two years. Calhoun's early education is still vivid in his mind five decades after the fact and he recalls:

"I went to the third grade twice an' was in the fourth for three weeks. Then I had to work with my daddy. He didn't have no education whatsoever. Now in the school classes here, I don't make a high number on my readin' an' writin'. I make a passin' mark, that's all. There's no need for me to tell a feller a lie."

Classroom facilities in an old graying bungalow surrounded by palmetto are pleasant but inadequate; Mrs. Williams is trying to teach reading to both an advanced class and beginners in the same room. The only white man is a half-deaf old farmer who sits apart and does not try to participate; he comes to qualify for his checks. There is an equally old Negro woman looking numbly at her book, sliding her eyes up to see if the teacher is watching. Her face is sly with pretence, her mind a knot that cannot unravel. But others are trying with a beautiful intensity. Those who are advanced read from a textbook about the absurdly complicated saga of a Mr. Heinz who wants to become a doctor and has already been a famous crook and concert pianist. It begins:

"Since all men are born equal all men are entitled to an equal education." [65]

An elderly black woman reads it smoothly but pronounces the word "eekel" and is patiently corrected, over and over again, by Mrs. Williams, trying in a few moments to disabuse her of a lifetime habit of speech. Finally, the word is mastered.

The other book is the story of Jo-Jo, a monkey. It has brightly colored drawings of him in a tree with a parrot and only three or four words in big print on each page. Mrs. Williams talks to the adults trying to read this first-grade book with the kindly yet firm insistence that a first-grade teacher would employ. And her pupils respond with effort.

"There's Jo-Jo in the tree," Mrs. Williams says. "And what does he like to do. What does it say there?"

"He—likes—clahmb," reads a 25-year-old woman in the class.

"Not 'clahmb.' Climb. Try it, honey."

"He—likes—to—clahmb."

Mrs. Williams sighs lightly; they try again and it is better; they go on.

Mr. Dawkins, who had been using the plane in the carpentry class, is next. His black forefinger, almost tanned by work and time, moves along the page, marking each word in the saga of Jo-Jo pronounced by the middle-aged farmer beside him. From time to time, he sneaks a look at his seat companion, like a child hoping that something from a bright student will rub off on him. Time has turned upside down. At fifty-eight he becomes what he could not be at nine. Now, he is on his own.

"This—is—Jo—Jo," he reads, pronouncing each "Jo" separately. He isn't cheating from memory. Mr. Dawkins, who once made it into the second or third grade before a cotton field called, is trying to learn to read.

"That's very good," says Mrs. Williams. "Now, what is he?"

"He—is—a—lit—tle . . ."

Mr. Dawkins shakes his head as if a shake might clear away the fogs of old ignorance.

"Well, now you can read what he is," says Mrs. Williams. "The word is right there."

Mr. Dawkins licks his lips and starts over with his finger. And something happens then to someone watching him. It suddenly becomes the most important thing in the world for Mr. Dawkins to tell what that damned Jo-Jo is.

Come on, say it, Mr. Dawkins. Prove that something good is happening to you for once in your life. Say it . . .

"Jo—Jo—is . . ."

A what?

"Jo-Jo—is—a—mon—key."

Right, Mr. Dawkins! Beautiful. We have at last one indisputable fact established in the nation's program to help its poor. Jo-Jo is a monkey. And Mr. Dawkins, tired-eyed, slump-backed, finger fumbling along the next line, Mr. Dawkins is a what?

He's a man.

12

Tales of Woe

OWEN WISTER relates a story told to him by Mark Twain about a missionary he heard preach one Sunday on the sufferings of some natives. Twain said the man preached so movingly that he mentally doubled the fifty cents he had intended to donate, raised the dollar to five as the pathetic tale continued, and, finally, reduced to tears, decided he would contribute a large check.

"And then that preacher went on," said Mark Twain. "Went on about the dreadful state of those natives. I abandoned the idea of the check. And he went on. And I got back down to five dollars, four, two, one. But he went on. And when the plate came around—I took ten cents out of it."

There is a similar risk when you write about poverty. There comes a point when the reader (even the writer) is tempted to say, enough is enough. Why more tales of woe when we have only so many coins of pity to spend? But because poverty is not simple in its causes or uniform in its results, different stories reveal different aspects of the problem and perhaps—only perhaps—point toward appropriate solutions. For example, there are two shacks in Lee County, Georgia, that might be visited without playing the spendthrift with inconsequential pity.

The first is visited during a shower that wets down a parched patch of collard greens, squash, and okra in the dusty front yard. The shack is worse than most, better than some, raised off the ground by stumpy brick pillars at the edge of a soybean field. Inside, rain beats on the galvanized roof and flies hang in the heavy air. The plank floor is clean-swept. There is a burned and rotting fireplace that looks as if it is devouring itself. The heavy air weights the odor of charred wood laced with urine. The furniture consists of six iron beds with bare mattresses. Children are all over the floor and the beds, but there is no other adult in the shack. A baby wrapped in a clean cotton blanket sleeps quietly on one splotched mattress. (That it might be an infant mortality statistic instead of a living baby is not immediately apparent.) A girl about four sits on an adjoining bed under a low rafter holding a baby bottle; her expression is torpid as she leans against a boy a few years older who slowly wipes flies from his face and smiles. He's holding a child's book called *Through the Green Gate*. The cover shows two white children, boy and girl, walking into a garden.

Jimmy Lee Smith, ten, speaks up to the visitor and says that his mother is out, his father is dead. There are sixteen children, and he will name them: there is Ramona, Bobby Jane, Otis, Artis, Larry John, Delphinia.... Larry John, nine, likes to talk, even to a stranger who asks personal questions about his health and Christmas. Last Christmas, he says, there were presents. He and his brothers and sisters received one gun and two trucks. His health is good.

"I ain't never went to a doctor," he says. "But I seen one once."

Jimmy Lee permits a look into the kitchen and the refrigerator. The refrigerator holds: two jars of Gerber's strained oatmeal, one squash, two plastic Clorox jugs filled with water, one bar of butter, one bag of black-eyed peas. That is all the food in the refrigerator or in the kitchen.

"What do you eat, Jimy Lee?"

"We eats—well—we eats okry, fatback, an' bread."

"Does the house have a privy out back?"

"No, suh."

"Is there a well?"

"No, suh."

"What do you do for water?"

"We fetch it from a church out back."

"Where?"

"Back yonder behind the field." [66]

The soybean field stretches for about a quarter of a mile, ending in a small woods with the church presumably just beyond—so far away that when one of the children goes to fetch water he is a black dot by the time he reaches the distant rim of the field. While Jimmy Lee chats, two girls in their early teens who at first had not been there sidle shyly in and out of the room. Younger children make fences of their fingers, peer from behind them and giggle. There is a lazing atmosphere of time suspended as flies hang in the air and the rain beats on the galvanized roof. The visitor tells Jimmy Lee that he will return next day to talk to his mama and Jimmy Lee smiles and says good-bye.

The next morning when the car rolls into the yard, Jimmy Lee charges out onto the porch brandishing a stick.

"Get outa here!" he yells. "You go now or I'll get me a shotgun. Goddamn white trash. Get off or my mama'll whop you ass good."

The arrival of his mother in a friend's car saves the day. Explanations are exchanged, and Jimmy Lee, smiling but unabashed, quiets down. A family conclave the night before had concluded that the uninvited white visitor was up to no good, probably come to make off with the teenage girls. Jimmy Lee had stepped into the man's role. His mother is hefty, taciturn, and not pleased with her unsolicited role as a poverty case history. But she grudgingly complies and her looks suggest the suspicion that the white talker might mean official trouble unless there were cooperation.

Five of the children, she says, are hers. Eight belong to her daughters, here and there, unmarried.[67] Three are from sisters living in New York. One daughter, Marie, mother of the baby, has arrived with her. Mrs. Smith is only thirty-three and so the ages of the daughters must begin with a subtraction of eighteen or so years. Mrs. Smith and Marie work on and off as domestics in Albany, earning $4.50 a day including 50 cents carfare, $20 take-home for a five-day week. Mrs. Smith dismisses an inquiry about welfare with a shake of the head.

"I don't wanna know nothin' about that," she says. "We don't take it." [68]

They have just returned from a week's shopping for two adults and sixteen children. The box holds: two chickens, four short ribs, two pounds of sausage, two pounds of fatback, one package of lard, two cans of sardines, one can of instant milk, a package of cornmeal, and a package of flour.

Lee County, with 50 percent poverty, had no federal food in 1967, and they have paid full price for the groceries, $20. There is another price being paid in that shack without a privy, without a well. The baby, Marie's daughter, had been born seven months before without an anus.

It is too much. The poor are stretching our sympathy to the breaking point and the moment for Twain's snort of irascibility has arrived. But the moment passes and there remains a small soul who would have died miserably in her first day if there hadn't been a white doctor in the Albany Hospital who saw the emergency and ordered an operating room opened without the customary $50 black deposit and saved the baby.

The baby, Angela, was saved at a price. The price at the hospital was $1,598. The mother, Marie Smith, eighteen and earning $22.50 a week, is supposed to pay $50 a month to the hospital *in addition to the doctor bill*. This totals nearly three weeks' salary and there is no agency willing to help her. At the same time, she is expected (by society, I suppose) to provide the baby with proper food, Pablum, formula, strained carrots— all the good things we spoon into an infant's mouth, anxious to see it consumed, our love consumed with it. At the same time, while working, she is expected to make sure that the baby with its grievous little wound is kept fresh and sanitary. Yes. With clean diapers at the ready. Yes. With young teenagers watching Angela and the well a quarter of a mile away, yes, Marie can surely do it. The county health service, the state board of health, the Federal Health Service—they count on her to provide for Angela and do not disturb her with the kind of surprise visits that welfare likes to make, searching for a cohabiting man who might be charged with nonsupport. Officialdom is concerned with who is in bed with whom; it is not concerned with whether there is water to wash out the diapers of Angela, born without an anus, child of our American century that produces one of the worst infant mortality rates recorded by "modern" nations.[69]

The other tale of woe is about Beverly Brown, six, who also lives in a Lee County shack. The shack is a grade better, but she is an inheritor of a common black portion: a father who still half-crops, a mother who chops and picks peas, an eighty-three-year-old grandmother whose parents were slaves, and numerous brothers and sisters, one brother in the Army. On December 5, 1966, Beverly was trying to keep warm before the only fireplace in the shack when her dress caught fire. Mrs. Brown says:

"You don't know where your trouble is comin' from, but you know it's comin'. Still, I thank God we was so lucky. The Lord fixed it so my mama was nearby. She beat out the flames or Beverly would've been gone."

Beverly remains, her back and buttocks burned so deeply that six months later the open flesh has just closed over. Mrs. Brown lifts the girl's dress to show the scarified mass where the beautiful black skin ends and the lumpy layers of tissue run together like melted wax.

"They did grafts," Mrs. Brown says. "But it wasn't too good. In the Leslie Clinic they got a real nice nurse. Best I ever seen. She wanted to send the baby to Atlanta for special treatment so it wouldn't look so bad. But somebody had to go with her an' we just didn't have the money. The cheapest hospital here cost us thirteen dollars a day an' the whole bill was six hundred and eighty. That don't count the doctor. He says this child needs vitamins an' fresh milk. I know she does. Don't you think I know she does? But the onliest milk I can buy is once a week. I tried for welfare but they couldn't give me none 'cause I had a husband."

Beverly sprawled in her mother's lap, arms around her neck, while Mrs. Brown lightly rubbed the scars and a lot of love passed back and forth.

"It's pathetic, that's what it is," the mother says. "I'm forty now but I wish I was sixty-two. Then I could go an' get a check an' wouldn't have to beg for money."

The particulars of Mrs. Brown's life by now are familiar and could be easily checked off by a welfare functionary with a little list: husband divides peanut crop with boss man first week in December and has to borrow for Christmas presents.

Check.

The Man's family gives the Browns clothes in the winter.

Check.

Mrs. Brown still chops cotton at $3 a day, her nine-year-old daughter Susan has to pay 25 cents a day for school lunch.

Check.

But some kind of double check has to be made on a society that can tolerate Beverly's burning, can continue getting and spending on December 5, 1966, and the days thereafter, instead of dropping everything to lift the scars and make her whole again. How many things that any nation can do on any given day could be any more important than repairing the damaged child Beverly? Mrs. Lyndon Johnson's highway and garden beautification program was budgeted at $85 million dollars. But will no one in government set a price of a few hundred or maybe a few thousand dollars to make a child's back comely in preparation for the day when she will be a young woman? Priority. A sense of seemliness that convinces a government to perfect a weapon sending air heated to 1,000 degrees into enemy tunnels in Vietnam, but cannot salve the scorched innocent at home.[70]

"I know it all ain't right," the mother says. "But what can you do?"

What Mrs. Brown does is to pray a good deal. In a dark and cluttered bedroom where five children sleep there is a motto hanging on the wall: Christ Is the Head of This House. (And, ironically rendering unto Caesar, on the plank floor by the bed of fourteen-year-old Shirley Ann, who is going to have to drop out of high school to go to work, is one of her civics books: *Building Citizenship*.) In the living room where Beverly was burned another motto hangs: Prayer Changes Things.

"I know it will change things," Mrs. Brown says. "So I keep on prayin'. God didn't say He was comin' for just the white *or* colored. An' God didn't say He'd come when *you* wanted him but when He knows it's needy time."

It is impossible to leave that shack and drive a few minutes down the highway to where a sign, in the name of the John

Birch Society, asks that Earl Warren be impeached to help save our country, impossible to see the sign and know what it signifies and at the same time to remember Beverly's back, impossible to do these things without concluding that—Mrs. Brown's patient faith to the contrary notwithstanding—the needy time is now.

13

Land Mismanaged to Catastrophe

POVERTY anywhere in the richest country on earth presents a paradox. In the Appalachian region of eastern Kentucky, the proportions of the paradox become unreal as penury lives next to fantastic wealth. The wealth is below ground, billions of tons of bituminous, or soft, coal controlled by multimillion-dollar corporations. Above it live some of the poorest white people (and a few blacks) in America. In Perry County, half the population is poor enough to qualify for free federal food. In Perry County, *one* mining combine holds a single contract for $100 million.

Unemployment in Perry County hovers around 15 percent.[71] This is not exceptional in an area containing ten of the twenty poorest counties in the United States. Over the line in Leslie County, nearly 35 percent of the men are unemployed.[72] You see them sitting on their shack porches in the verdant hills and hollows characteristic of the Cumberland plateau, men leaning on their elbows, looking out at the two-lane highway where coal trucks roar by, bearing away the region's patrimony and leaving in their exhaust despair that has come to stay. In towns with names like Vico, Scuddy, Defiance, Mousie, and Boon Ledge, children are held back by pride from going to school because they have no shoes. Their fathers usually are former coal miners, the majority drained of health in midlife by diseases inevitable for those who remain long enough in the mines— silicosis, tuberculosis, arthritis, and, a touch of Madison Avenue for Caliban in his coal mine,[73] stomach ulcers, possibly caused by the combination of stress and poor diet. Many of these men are mutilated, looking for all the world like inmates of old-time leper colonies, with joints of fingers, hands, arms, and legs lopped off in accidents that were not so much an occupational hazard as they were an occupational certainty.

The men have the numbed air of those who do not know what hit them. Their bewilderment is understandable. In 1950, in that same Leslie County where 35 percent are unemployed (500 of 1,500 work-age men), the unemployment rate of 2.4 percent was close to the lowest in the nation. The same little towns that now are gray and hungry were bright with prosperity, a prosperity, however, that was measured from one pay-day to the next, and totally dependent on a mineral version of the Black Belt's one-crop economy. Coal was the crop, miners the tenants and hired hands, corporations were the Man. And then, almost overnight, the paydays stopped. Automation started, just as the mechanical cotton harvester and six-row tractor and chemical weed killers started in one day, it seemed, or two at most in Deep South fields.

Blanket apologists for automation, prophets of the bountiful millennium it will produce, should be sentenced to eastern Kentucky for a year. They would see this American Dream turned to nightmare, men reduced to paupery by machines enriching only distant boards of directors and stockholders. In an era of national concern over crime in the streets and riotous looting (social and economic grief turned to madness) crimes in the Cumberland hills go undenounced except by a few men, like Harry Caudill, the brave and brilliant Kentucky writer who told a Senate committee [74] in June, 1967:

> For three quarters of a century, Appalachia, including eastern Kentucky, powered America. The nation's growth and prosperity rested on bituminous coal—the primer fuel for ships, locomotives, factories and power plants.[75] But while Appalachian coal did much for America, it did little for Appalachia. Very little of the wealth it generated stayed in the area. And, following the old pattern, it still flows out by pipelines, trains and trucks in a ceaseless flood of dividend checks. Extractive industries make only trifling contributions to local services and facilities. Their

taxes are little more than nominal. They have brought tax
avoidance to near perfection. The counties richest in mineral
wealth make the smallest contribution to their schools.[76] Originally, the hills contained 35 billion tons of coal and now after
55 years of mining nearly 33 billion tons remain.... [But] this
rich land has been mismanaged to catastrophe.

The committee listened and did nothing. The evidence pre-
sented to it showed clearly and simply that numbers of Americans were poor in the midst of wealth. The late Sen. Robert
Kennedy once observed that "a number of our corporations are
making profits greater than seventy of the countries of the
world." Yet some of these corporations, like Ford, U.S. Steel, and
Republic Steel, are involved in eastern Kentucky, and their kind
of power always complicates reform. In addition to automation of existing mines, the new and inhuman factor of strip
mining was added. It is a process needing only a handful of
men to run giant machines that carve up entire mountains,
scraping coal from the surface without laborious, costly tun-
neling, and creating handsome profits and enormous devasta-
tion.[77] And it insured that the labor force of the fifties would
no longer be needed. As Buck Sims and tenant farmers like
him became expendable, so did mining families that had dug
for generations in Appalachia. Corporation computers whirled:
so many machines required so few men to make so much profit.
Men accordingly were cast on a human slag heap. The federal
government did not make a single legislative move to help.
The United Mine Workers Union, whose former leader had
been a demigod to miners, was criminally negligent of members who had paid into pension funds for decades and who, at
a time of need, were roundly rebuffed with evasions and tech-
nicalities when they tried to collect. The union wasn't poor. In
fact, it had turned into big business, big and peculiar business.
On August 24, 1967, with thousands of ex-miners destitute, the
UMW was found guilty in federal court of making massive
loans to a *Kentucky coal company* to help it monopolize TVA
contracts and drive two Tennessee firms out of business.[78]

One end product of all these machinations is fifty-five-year-
old John Weltner, who spent twenty-two years in the mines
and lives in a shack with his family outside the county seat of

Hyden in Leslie County. The setting is typical eastern Kentucky, the hills lush with green where strip mining has not scarified them. Abundant rainfall saturates the ground and water trickles continuously down rock faces alongside the narrow road, the road dipping into damp hollows where the sensation is one with a bug in a bush, green pressing on all sides and up the pine hills that fold back on themselves, closing off all horizons. The pocketed air is green except in the remote blue sky. A visitor to the hills feels security and isolation, entrapment and freedom. Here and there in a clearing are the blackened timbers of a ruined tipple, where coal used to be rolled down on mine cars for loading onto trucks, the sagging railway scaffolding standing like an abandoned roller coaster.

Weltner's shack is near such a tipple. Outside, by a garden of potatoes, beans, cabbages, and onions, there is a line of wash hanging clean as a detergent ad; it is a mark of pride with mountain housewives to hang a line every day except Sunday. This labor of love is more difficult for Mrs. Weltner than for most; despite the region's abundance of water, the shack does not have a pump, and like the Fergursons of Bainbridge, Georgia, the family must cross the road to get water from a neighbor. With five children to scrub for, there is a lot of bucket traffic on the road. Weltner is a skinny, walleyed man with a vague stare who looks like one of the walking wounded in a war newsreel.

"I got busted in half in the mines," he says. "Back broke, eyes shot. One weren't good to begin with. You can see. I used to draw fifty dollars a month pension but a year or so ago they said they lost the papers and I never been able to get it going again. With five younguns in school I had to get somethin'. They started up this Work Experience program which I got into for four months. Around here we call it the Happy Pappies.[79] Then I heard of a mine job that might be openin' so I took a trip to Harlan to see if I could pass the eye test to go back in. I flunked but when I got back here from Harlan they said the time I was gone disqualified me for the Work Experience. Which may be true, I don't really know. I drew my last program check five months ago and now I'm takin' the state blind examination to see if I can get a pension there."

John Weltner is blind in one eye and has 30 percent vision in the other. He does not find anything remarkable in first trying to get certified to work in a coal mine and a few months later trying to be certified as blind. His story, except for this desperate specific, is remarkably similar to many a visitor hears in the hills. Even his fifth-grade education is close to the county median—not average—of 6.9 years.[80]

"Fifteen years ago we could make good money here," he says. "Then it all went. And now, if it wasn't for the food stamps and the fact I raise me a pretty good garden we'd be up against it bad.[81] Stamps are good except they just don't last out the month. After about three weeks they're gone and then you borrow all the time. But you gotta put somethin' in their stomachs when they're goin' off to school, don't you?"

A grown son stands beside him, James Weltner, a dark-haired young man of twenty-one with collegiate good looks who dropped out of school in the eighth grade to go into the mines. Now he is married and has two children but there is no job to go to.

"You just go out lookin' an' hopin' to snatch one here or there," he says. "Sure, I'd like to do somethin' else. But I know I can't without an education. The way I look at mining is, if you get busted up like my daddy you don't get much out of it. But if you get killed, at least your family gets a chunk of money to do 'em for a while."

Tides of self-defeatism, romantic fatalism, and pride run in these mountaineers and mix in young Weltner's "philosophy." Strength and weakness sweep in on those psychological tides. Basically, they render men vulnerable to forces that are more deliberate and controlled; under pressure of these corporate forces, flight is often the mountaineer's recourse, extending the parallel to the Black Belt, where Negroes flee what they cannot come to terms with, psychologically or materially. The mountaineers, not racially ostracized, not burdened with inferior and hateful self-images and thus capable of forging bonds of mutual esteem in a unity of need, still have little more resistance than the Mississippi black tenant when the economic screws are tightened. Leslie County's population dropped 30 percent between 1950 and 1960. Neighboring Letcher County, with the same kind of problems, has dropped from 44,000 to 24,000 during this century. A University of Kentucky survey indicates that during the present decade the population of the region will drop from 884,000 to 723,000. In the pattern of the Southern exodus, it is the young and vigorous who are leaving, the old who are remaining to die: Leslie County's death rate has nearly doubled between 1950 and 1963, while the birth rate dropped.[82]

On a rainy day in the city of Hazard, some people trying to challenge eastern Kentucky's legacy of misery met in the make-shift OEO office. It is housed in a turn-of-the-century hospital about to be torn down, but in one way the location is appropriate. The office is in the old emergency waiting room. A straight-talking mountain man named Everett Tharp who runs the county program knows an emergency when he sees one; he also knows when it isn't being met. Tharp says:

"What I'd like to see—but don't see—is a broad, comprehensive manpower plan for the four LKLP counties, something like the WPA. Give heavy-equipment training, teach 'em a trade, let 'em have a steady paycheck that won't disappear with the next appropriation. Maybe that way they can get their self-respect back—because they feel it, doing nothing, no matter how proud they talk—and leave here trained to do something except mine coal. Leave, yes. There are long-range plans for highways [83] to come in here and dams to be built. But that's a far way off if it ever comes."

Mrs. Vista Grigsby [84] is the only OEO social aid worker in Perry County with 32,000 people, half of whom are poor enough to receive federal food.[85] Mrs. Grigsby is supposed to help bed-ridden poor people get doctors and medicine,[86] give food preparation training to stamp recipients, aid the qualified in securing welfare, find legal channels for ex-miners continually "lawing" with the union or Workmen's Compensation to get fair exchange for a leg or twenty-five years in the pits. Her nature is charitable, but she never uses the word "charity" nor would she condone its use. A gray-haired, spare woman, her sympathies and frustrations are equally obvious.

"So many of the people around here have tried many times to improve their condition," she says. "They have tried many times to get jobs and have failed because there are none. It's pathetic because they no longer have the hope that trying will succeed.

"I'm from the mountains and spent a greater part of my life in social work. We have many families that aren't getting enough food. Some are desperate because they can only obtain a minimum of social security. Some are in between social security and welfare, and can't get enough of either. They live on peas, potatoes, and cornbread. Some of the children get at least one decent meal a day in school. But it's left up to the principal who he feeds and who doesn't get it. So he has to look at the hungry faces and decide which eats. In the one-room schoolhouses, there aren't cooking facilities so the children don't even get that. Things here in eastern Kentucky could break your heart."

Was a special food program needed for the children?

"The best program for the children," says Tharp, "would be a job for the father of the house."

The rain runs gray on the window and figures pass on the sloping sidewalk; Hazard is built on hills and everything is up or down. Tharp and Mrs. Grigsby describe the last "training" program conducted by the Labor Department agency. Out of hundreds of applicants only thirty-four men could be accepted for want of funds. For eight weeks, they said, the men were taught how to fill out job questionnaires (when there were no jobs), how to dress (when they had no money to buy clothes), and how to fill out income tax forms (when some hadn't made a taxable dollar in ten years).

"These were men with hungry families who couldn't get on welfare because they were technically employable," Mrs. Grigsby says. "Some were over sixty. It was good that they were getting some money. But once the program ended they were going to be right back where they started. I think better programs could be developed with county help. But the county won't contribute because it says it doesn't have it. Still, with all that coal coming out . . . There's so much work could be done if we had some backing. There's strip mine land to be reclaimed, hospitals to be built, housing, schools. We're still using schools built by the WPA and they were good ones. But the present programs, I have to say, are really doing nothing to benefit this country."

There are many apparent similarities between poor white Kentuckians and poor black Alabamians or Georgians. But there is one important difference. Or two, in Perry County. People like Tharp and Mrs. Grigsby. In her mouth, words like social work aren't dry and bitter but sweet with concern for people. Tharp, faced with great problems and small means, knows he is outclassed; but he wants to prevail. Where so many Deep South Poverty offices are little internecine battlefields—whites guarding ancient prerogatives, blacks struggling for a voice proportionate to need—the Hazard office is one with the people it serves against the common enemy. The enemy is amorphous, it is not black. It is made up of those stupefyingly powerful public and private forces whose shapes blend into the figure called the Establishment or the Power Structure, adept at taking away much and giving back little, tolerant of or indifferent to the sight of a generation of men leaning on their elbows and watching the cars go by. And even when this amorphous enemy seems to move toward a truce, a just peace, the Hazard office and the people dependent on it find that it is a trick, luring men from their shacks with a promissory note of hope, so that they squeeze their rough frames into children's classroom seats and watch as a man comes in and teaches them—income tax forms.

14

The Hearing

THE poor often go unheard, sometimes because they don't speak up, often because no one who is not poor wants to listen. Heywood Broun reportedly remarked while watching a Depression breadline:

"Poor people wouldn't be such a bother if they didn't starve so publicly."

That may have been true in the thirties. But today's poor are mostly tucked away out of the common sight, in black ghettos, small rural towns, or mountain communities filled— like isolation wards—with poverty's most woebegone inmates. The government sometimes cocks an ear to the stories of the poor but the government, after all, is principally made up of men who are not poor, who have never been poor, and who do not owe their positions to any power or pressure exerted by a minority class whose fragmentation renders it politically powerless despite the ballot and whose lack of money insures it cannot mount pressure in a society basically responsive to the force of dollars. So the minions of government listen with a mixture of impatience, condescension, and inattentiveness when the poor try to address them, preferring to consider statistics— emotionally undemanding and qualitatively vague for all their precision—when they consider the poor at all. The resultant programs are financed by shaving off a sliver from the 23 percent of the national budget remaining after the Defense Department gets through with it. The money is doled out in accordance with variable standards of expediency which usually bear little or no relation to the individual lives on the receiving end of the dole.

It is left by default to private groups like the Citizens Crusade Against Poverty (CCAP) [87] to listen closely and with compassion to the poor in an effort to learn whether they are sick or hungry, whether their children are getting educated or absorbing ignorance, as their parents did, and whether state and federal assistance programs are doing any constructive good or merely creating a fiction of social reform. The economic and human history of eastern Kentucky makes it an appropriate place to raise such questions, so on August 22, 1967, a Board of Inquiry into Hunger and Malnutrition called by CCAP held a hearing in the meeting hall of UMW Local 5890, a once-white frame building grimy from the coal cars that have rolled for decades along the railroad tracks fifty yards away.

For weeks, the Appalachian Volunteers, a privately endowed organization, had been asking the mountain poor with whom they worked to come to testify. At the last minute, plans for the hearing almost came apart at the seams. On August 18, OEO Director Sargent Shriver gave the order mentioned in note 84 that cut all funds to the Volunteers because of the purported seditious activity of one Volunteer named Joe Mulloy.[88] Confusion and suspicion settled in the hollows. To many unsophisticated minds, accusation signified guilt. Certain politicians and coal mining interests encouraged this assumption. Yet, on the morning of the hearings, mountain people flocked into Hazard to tell their stories and praise the Volunteers.

Before the hearing began, a sixty-year-old ex-miner from Wolfpit in Pike County, Harry Burnside, sat outside the UMW hall and summed up—in his person and through his unsolicited reflections—what the day was all about. Stumps of fingers held a cigarette in the moss-cool mountain air as he talked, his voice as rough as a coal augur.

"Them AV's was doin' a fine job, an' they're fine people, that's all. Same with the VISTA's [Volunteers In Service To America, the domestic version of the Peace Corps]. They been fixin' up a schoolhouse near us to teach the poor kids. Two girls stayed at the house alongside me an' they was the finest girls

I ever seen. Nothin' out of the way. Help a sick lady with her wash, watch kids, pitch right in on dirty jobs, do anything to help out. Two of the boys stayed with us an' they was the same type.

"Some people got scared to death about comin' here today when Joe Mulloy got arrested. One feller went aroun' sayin' the AV's was bringin' in a bunch of niggers an' Communists. But all Joe ever did was try to get poor people to figger out what they should do. I saw him. Don't I know? Most people see it right an' they got a petition goin' to give Joe support. But there's others . . . I get so mad."

He ground out the cigarette on the step. Burnside's face held more disgust than anger, a face still busy with emotional involvement despite his years, a miner's face dusted with coal particles from buried seams that had surfaced in his broad pores and remained there.

"The strip minin' business is what's stirrin' it all up," he says. "The AV's wasn't for it. Well sure, why should they be? It tears the land off the mountains, washes it down, scrapes a road forty foot wide aroun' the mountains. What are they gonna put back? It took almost five hundred trees above one farm near me till the woman got out with a shotgun an' run 'em off. They'll come back with the law. An' people like us, we ain't got money for the law.[89] But you can just bet they'll come back. Two men runs the augur, shifts day an' night, an' they take out eight hundred ton in eight hours. Figure it at five dollar a ton. Just figure it."

Burnside worked in the mines for thirty-seven years and once stayed out on a UMW strike for eighteen months. No scab in Harry Burnside. But when hard times came to the hills he, along with other miners, took jobs where he could find them. Some were in nonunion pits and this gave the UMW its excuse to deny him a pension. It is a story commonplace in eastern Kentucky (part of the un-simplicities of poverty), and Burnside told it without rancor. The union "hoaked me"; it was just the way things were. The same with his hands. Burnside answered questions about the missing digits in a detached way, almost as if the hands and their segments were products he offered up for sale. Those two fingers off his left hand . . .

"Rock fell on them. Eighteenth day of October, 1962. But I didn't get much out of it, a few hundred only. Now I got fifty dollars for the *end* of this one"—he held up the bare base of what once had been the index finger on his right hand—"but when they got the last two joints it was eight hundred. Them other two joints alongside the next finger I couldn't get a thing for." He shook his head with a half smile. "I been hurt so bad so many times I don't remember."

His mutilations have earned Burnside an $80.30 monthly social security disability payment. Eight dollars comes out of that for food stamps for him and his wife. The stamps were cut off this summer when two AV's stayed in his shack paying $15 a week for room and board. Burnside thinks this was an arbitrary decision but he didn't know of any way to appeal it and so he made do without the stamps until the boys left. He shrugs and goes inside to see the only free show on poverty in the memory of Kentucky mountain men.

Inside, the hall is clean and Spartan, with rows of benches, where working coal miners once sat, awaiting ex-miners and other mountain people come to observe and testify. A workmanlike painting of John L. Lewis glowers benignly from the wall above the heads of the CCAP panel.[90] Co-chairman Leslie Dunbar rises to read a telegram of welcome from Kentucky Republican Senator Sherman Cooper.

"I want to do all I can to be of assistance," the senator had wired. "And to take whatever appropriate legislative action is necessary." [91]

With that pledge recorded, witnesses begin making their record of poverty in the hills.

Witness: Homer Pierce of Darfolk Hollow, Perry County. Stocky, voluble for a mountain man, his gray-blue eyes frosty with complaint. He has testified once in Washington and has the assurance of an old pro.

Statistics: Thirty-four, with a second-grade education, a wife and nine children, ages two to sixteen. Worked seventeen years in the mines but receives no UMW pension. Gets $84 worth of food stamps for $3 yet has no income with which to buy them. Welfare gives nothing because he is technically able to work. A year-long Happy Pappies veteran until his time in the program expired. Last drew a poverty paycheck in June from a "pre-vocational" program.

Testimony: "We can live pretty good on stamps until the end of the second week, then we stretch with rough stuff. Milk for the kids? They're lucky to have it twice a month. I won't say they're hungry, though. But I have four to start in school and can't start 'em for lack of clothes. That's a hard thing for a man to say but it's the Gospel truth. We live on credit after the stamps run out. But the trouble is my credit's run out except for a few relatives who manage a couple of dollars now and then.... I quit the mines in 1959. They starved us out, givin' ten dollars a shift cuttin' coal from three in the afternoon till four next mornin'.... On government programs I have to say that they give a man some money but they don't do any good. Happy Pappies was just go out and cut brush, do roadwork but no real training. And that pre-vocational wasn't nothin' but a big bunch of foolishness. They had ten teachers for thirty-four men, talkin' about stuff that a man with no education couldn't understand. I've seen plenty of stuff that was worthless but this was *worthless*. Why they even showed Civil War movies, hillbilly bands, and a picture about Casey Jones."

A pre-vocational work card is produced. The course for chronically unemployed men consisted of: 42 hours—Qualifying for Employment, 66 hours—Job Orientation Analysis, 28 hours —Labor Management, 16 hours—Safety Education, 32 hours— Mathematics Orientation, 36 hours—Automation and Future Employment, 30 hours—Fringe Benefits.

Witness: Mrs. Damon Jordan, Floyd County. A gaunt woman in a long green dress and blue sneakers, she is uneasy being on display but gains confidence and under questioning tells a straightforward story.

Statistics: About forty-five, married with six children from seven to eighteen and a husband too sick to work. Four children are in school. The family receives $82 worth of food stamps for $3. The $3 comes from charitable neighbors in a county very badly off.[92] Welfare gives nothing.

Testimony: "Well there's just no cash income at all. Mr. Jordan suffers with his heart and ulcers, and he plain can't work. Though they say he can. The state has sent him to two or three doctors an' they claim he can do light work. Even if he could, there isn't any but the welfare says they can't give us anything because he can work. Occasionally somebody lets him get out a ton of house coal but it just about kills him.

"He was in the Happy Pappies for four months last year. Then the children got sick with mumps an' jaundice. I doctored them an' when they went back the school said they needed a doctor's note. Which I didn't have because I didn't have a doctor. So then they dropped my husband off the program as a punishment for keepin' the children out of school. Which wasn't fair at all. . . . Those children aren't gettin' the right food, I know. Hardly ever get fresh milk. If it wasn't for our garden, we'd have to do without as the stamps don't possibly last with eight of us at the table. The children in school can get a lunch at fifteen cents apiece but we just don't have the fifteen cents. As to how I'll do this winter for those children, I *know* what I'm a-gonna do. I'm a-gonna get a pick an' dig out coal."

The hearing later receives evidence from Dr. Jorge Deju, director of the Kentucky Health Department's division of Maternal and Child Health. A 1955-1956 study showed that only 16 percent of children surveyed received the needed amount of green and yellow vegetables for proper nutrition while 61 percent *got none at all.* Thirty-two percent of the children ate the needed amount of citrus fruit while 47 percent never had an orange, grapefruit, or lemon throughout the year.

George Archer, Pike County coroner for eight years, from 1954 to 1961, testifies—although he is not a doctor—that the death certificates of twenty-four children dead on arrival at hospitals during that period listed malnutrition as the cause.

The audience takes it all in soberly. Many are friends and relatives of the witnesses; they nod occasionally at testimony their experience verifies and their faces show no shock at even the most dire tales. A young, fat reporter for the Hazard *Herald* does not take notes as Mrs. Mary Hadley tells how she had to "law with the state insurance people" to collect $1,900 when her son was killed in a mine. Mrs. Billie Jeffries, a widow with six children, including a twenty-year-old retarded son, says she built her house with the few thousand paid for her oldest son's

life, lost in the mines; she and his brothers and sisters live in the
dearly purchased house on $38 a week welfare. Joseph Peters, a
miner for twenty-three years, describes how coal companies
change names and locations to avoid lawsuits by miners seeking damages for mine accidents or pension consideration. Mrs.
Luke Tennyson, with eight children, keeps gettting cut off
welfare because welfare doctors insist that her husband can
work while *his* doctor says he "might last a day, might last a
month" if he went back down, suffering as he is from pernicious
anemia, a damaged heart, bone disease, and a lung growth that
"smothers him till it feels like his lungs are full of water."

The clash of coal cars coupling outside punctuates the recita-
tions of fast and slow death in the mines, hunger, disease, eva-
sion of responsibility by company and union, capricious welfare, inadequate food stamps. A listener from the outside world
becomes numbed at the doleful sameness, does not wish to hear
any more medical histories scrawled in bituminous coal, wonders if his reaction is what happens to welfare workers who end
up despising those who burden their souls with case histories
of sorrow and need. A break in the hearing is welcome. The
Crusade distributes box lunches, gravely received by witnesses
and spectators, who carefully do not hurry to the line, who accept with prideful courtesy, who eat some of the fried chicken
and then discretely close the box and keep it beside them. A
swarthy man about forty with eyes like coal smudges sits on a
slope of scraggly grass outside the hall, picking—pickin'—at a
guitar, singing unselfconsciously in a screech owl voice inter-
minable choruses about dank and doomed mountain love. Much
soda pop is drunk; eastern Kentucky has the highest consump-
tion rate of carbonated beverages in the United States. Appar-
ently there is a reward factor beyond thirst in a dime dope that
offers rare material self-indulgence like the other luxury of a
deep inhale on a cigarette.

When the hearing resumes and the next witness is listed from
Letcher County, the listener braces for the inevitable because
the county is a statistical mess,[93] and only another messy tale
could proceed from it. And so it does. But there is something
in the teller that picks up all the previous ragged threads of

testimony and weaves them into the truth of what being poor means to a man.

John B. Cooney looks about fifty as he sits to testify, shirttail out over soiled khakis, frayed low-cut sneakers and no socks, skin taut and sallow, thinning hair, and hollows under his eyes, eyes a sick gray. They are the kind of eyes you prefer to look away from, not that they beg, for they are beyond begging, but because you know there is no restorative you can give them.

Dunbar proceeds gently with the questions necessary to establish destitution, and Cooney responds in a voice without resilience. He has a wife and four children, from nine to seventeen ... last worked the mines in 1958 ... presently has no income and only has a roof because a farmer lets him use a shack rent-free in exchange for keeping an eye on things. Cooney buys $70 worth of food stamps when he can rustle up $3, and in the past VISTA workers gave him the money when no one else would. He has tuberculosis, a bad heart, and a kidney condition that doctors fear might be cancer. He receives no UMW pension and cannot get on welfare.

"I was gettin' it from '60 to '62," he says. "But then they said I was well enough to work. I went back to the TB hospital an' they said I wasn't no weller than last time. But the welfare doctor, he said the other way. I put in again four months ago but I ain't heard."

Dunbar asks about the Happy Pappies program.

"I tried," Cooney replies. "But they told me I couldn't get on that because I was too sick."

Too sick for the Poverty Program, too well for welfare, Cooney symbolizes a word that his third-grade education does not permit him to understand—expendable. But if, no longer young or productive, he can be written off by authority, what about his children? Politicians high and low like to refer to children as the citizens of tomorrow. How was future citizenship faring in the Cooney family? Well, he explains, food and clothes are the big problems. There's never fresh milk but the family keeps a garden and on a diet of pinto beans, potatoes, bacon, baloney, and flour gravy, the children aren't about to starve.

"Do the children ever go hungry?" asks panel member Dr. James Carter of Vanderbilt University.

"Yes, sir," Cooney replies. "They do."

American children are not supposed to be thriving simply because they aren't starving. That is a lot in life allocated to Indians, certain South Americans, and other backward people; American children are supposed to flourish beyond the minimal accomplishment of not dying of hunger. John Cooney's children aren't.

"They all love school," he testifies, "but they been let down so much with clothes an' all. . . . They can't dress like the other kids an' it hurts 'em. Sometimes they can't go. I spent five days in jail last winter because I couldn't send 'em out." [94]

Cooney stops. His eyes glisten and he swallows down what is in his throat.

"I think the older ones are goin' to drop out," Cooney continues. "They have to ask other kids for pencils an' that gets old pretty quick. My daughter—she's seventeen—told me, 'If we had something to go on so my name wouldn't be on the bulletin board all the time for school fees, then I'd stay.' "

Cooney folds his hands in his lap and waits for another question. But the panel does not choose to further lacerate his self-esteem in that hall where miners once came together in days when there was purpose in the air and it was not unreasonable to believe that labor could be fairly exchanged for an orderly life where children went fed to school and fathers did not go to jail for keeping ill-clad sons and daughters home in the mountain winter. Cooney is excused. He starts to get up but there is something he would clarify.

"I don't want people to think I'm tryin' to look like the only man with troubles," he says. "There's people back in the hills sicker than I am. Poor as I am, too. An' they need help."

Later that afternoon, when the last witness is heard and the hearing ends, the young man who has been reporting the event for the Hazard *Herald* stands on the porch chatting with another writer. His article has already appeared. Oddly, with the stories of dozens of witnesses to choose from, he has devoted almost his entire story to a private interview with the first witness, Homer Pierce. Pierce appears as a lazy, truculent and ungrateful symbol of mountain poor, suspicious of the Appalachian Volunteers and antagonistic to the concept of the Poverty Program. The reporter is neatly dressed, obviously well-fed, and highly exasperated.

"These people," he says, "you have to live here to understand them. They say they don't give their children milk more than two or three times a month. Now that's a big bunch of bull. Most of them wouldn't know enough to provide milk if they had a thousand dollars. They're ignorant about proper diet and they don't want to learn. There's jobs to be found hereabouts if they'd look. Some people are working, aren't they, so there must be jobs. But they're independent. They want to do just what they want to do, live in the old mountain way their daddies did. They get a few dollars and they spend it on smokes and liquor. I *know* them. They don't really want anything better and and that's the truth of it."

The words spoken by the reporter about certain eastern Kentuckians had a familiar ring; the listener had heard them time and time again in latitudes a few degrees south. To the south, "they" were of another American clan who historically did not want anything better. Most poor white eastern Kentuckians would indignantly deny any kinship with that Southern clan. Yet they were clearly one brotherhood, as the Hazard reporter could point out: people who hated to work, loved to complain, and were content to watch their children go hungry.

15

Of Hookworms and Spanish Moss

POVERTY is hung with Spanish moss on the South Carolina coast. The scrim of moss draped on oak and cypress softens the landscape, creating romantic twilights and primeval mornings when fog lifts out of the swamps and mixes with the haze of smoke from shack chimneys. While the physical edge of South Carolina poverty is thus obscured, it is there, sharp and cutting. It is the second-poorest state in the Union with per capita income only a few dollars ahead of Mississippi. While Mississippi is not notably tender in its concern for the poor, all its counties participate in either the commodities or food stamp programs. No South Carolina county welcomes commodities and the state's overall record in helping poor families to eat is the worst in the nation.[95]

These figures might surprise tourists disporting themselves on picturesque Hilton Head Island in Beaufort County, where single rates in motels on the edge of the sparkling ocean start at $30 a day without meals. They might also be surprised to learn that some of the chambermaids whose anonymous brown faces are part of the scenery make $20 for a five-day week, while others who make slightly more were trained for their jobs with federal tax money under antipoverty programs designated to teach the poor new skills.

Black is the color of the worst poverty in Beaufort, which, with neighboring Jasper County, is one more fragment in the pile loosely swept into the national corner reserved for Economic Opportunity programs.[96] Beaufort, in many ways, is more fortunate than other South Carolina counties; playing the game of comparative poverty in the South can be a comfort since there is always somebody worse off down the line. Beaufort unemployment is officially only 5 percent, although cautionary skepticism would require a head count on any given workday before that figure could be trusted. There are the motels, a shrimp and canning industry, seasonal produce handling, and the Parris Island Marine Base, which has reflected the blessings of the Vietnam war in some civilian job increases. Still, things are tough and sometimes primitive.

A doctor who has been practicing in the area for eight years says that it has the highest parasitic infestation in America— roundworms, hookworms, and others more exotic, which thrive under unsanitary conditions and lodge inside human intestines and organs, particularly those of the young.[97] They can cause anemia and weaken the body's resistance to a host of other diseases; there is even evidence that IQs are markedly affected in children debilitated over the years by parasites. The doctor claims that since 1959 he has treated nine patients whose deaths were attributable to parasites.

"If that many were dying from polio in the county," he says, "Washington would have investigating teams down here from the National Institute of Health. But these are poor people who die quietly and so nothing is done."

His charge is impossible for the layman to verify without the kind of investigation requiring the competence of trained medical probers. But evidence of execrable sanitary conditions and chancy health services abound, some only a few minutes' drive from the plush motels of Hilton Head. There are numerous shacks to choose from, which, after a night's rain, are ringed by puddles where barefoot children slosh. One large and nominally dilapidated shack near Bluffton has a small lagoon splashing with black children in front. It is an appealing scene for a citified adult who recalls forbidden excursions into the mud of his childhood. But that mud was clean. This mud surrounds a house without an indoor or an outdoor toilet; the whole yard is a privy for humans and for chickens and for a hog penned on a rise that permits his private muck to wash down with the rest. Eventually the water will seep into the ground; eventually it will be brought up from the well and consumed.

There is a five-year-old boy inside this particular shack who is suffering from chronic diarrhea. He belongs to Mrs. Sara Rollins, who has five other children. She lives there with a woman she calls her sister-daughter, who has four children. There is also a younger woman named Mary Benton, who is twenty-nine and has five children, the eldest fifteen. The exact relationships are difficult to establish, but it is a matriarchal shack with no men in sight. Mrs. Rollins and her sister-daughter look alike; both are about forty-five and extremely fat. They sprawl on couches in a cheerfully rundown living room decorated with porcelain gimcrackery, sewing bright cloth patches for quilts while children and chickens wander in and out. The women, barefoot, are immobile as two old brown Buddhas except for their great hands, which pick small silver scissors from their laps and delicately snip, then sew, squares of white, blue, and cerise.

"Everybody's pretty healthy but Marvin Kenneth," Mrs. Rollins says. "When he gets real bad he goes to the state hospital in Charleston. They treats him fine an' he feels better but when he comes home he don't feel good. The doctors up there say it's the water. They ask me if I have runnin' water an' I say I can't afford to have pipes laid in to connect up with the system.[98] All I make except for sewin' is twenty-five dollars a week from September to May in the oyster cannin' factory. County won't do nothin'. Say my brother owns the house, he has to do it. But he's away an' ain't got it anyway. Marvin Kenneth, he's doin' poorly today. It comes with a pain in his stomach an' I go to rub it till he sleeps. He sleeps most of the time. It gets so after a while his skin you can pluck right up, it's so loose. Then they puts him back in the hospital with the glucose an' he feels better. Then he comes home an' starts to nasty up all the time."

An older sister brings in Marvin Kenneth. He looks like a child sick over and over again. He sneezes and sniffles; his eyes are washed out. He leans against his mother, a fragile hand dreamily pawing a cerise scrap. Mrs. Rollins does not boil his water; she says that no one at the hospital ever told her to. Has anyone ever come to test the water, somebody from the U.S. Public Health Service perhaps? No, nobody comes. From no place.[99] What is she going to do with Marvin Kenneth? Put him back in the hospital when he gets bad, she guesses. Mrs. Rollins' attitude toward the boy is not detached; she gives him a heavy hug; she does not want him to suffer, to die. But her own social metabolism is low. Life has accustomed her to situations that, however tragic, have to be endured. Poverty intimidates her; ignorance inhibits her from seeking out all possible sources of assistance; and the problem of what to do with Marvin Kenneth becomes just too much. This does not excuse her from responsibility. But her share of the blame—*or* of the excuses accruing from her circumstance—is irrelevant to the fact that Marvin Kenneth may be dying, with society unable or unwilling to do anything about it. Watching his lacklustre eyes as he toys with the scrap, one feels certain that he will someday go to the well once too often and that the culprit will not be hookworm, roundworm, or amoeba but something of a higher order of development.

Mrs. Rollins says that everyone except the boy is "pretty healthy," but this is a relative, maternal, expression. A daughter, Susan, looks like a twelve- or thirteen-year-old, slightly underweight. She turns out to be seventeen, a junior in Bluffton High School who would "kinda like to be a nurse" although no one in school ever discusses vocation with her. Susan suffers from a common complaint among rural poor which they call "low blood" and which is usually some form of anemia. At seventeen, she is a doe-eyed, listless brown bag of bones who explains that the doctor at the county clinic where she has her school checkup tells her she should have vitamin pills regularly. She *does* use them when he gives them to her. How often does she see him? Twice a year. How long do the pills last? Two weeks.

Mary Benton, the younger woman, says that most of her children are in good health despite the suspect water. One young son did have a hernia operation the previous month. He came out all right but the bill is something else. The hospital cost $152, the doctor $50. She paid $12 down and is paying off the rest from her bimonthly salary of $97 earned as a chambermaid at a Hilton Head motel. She receives $1 an hour and works a fifty-hour week. She can get no public assistance in South Carolina for her illegitimate children. The state's welfare law generally denies assistance to unwed mothers except in dire emergencies. Such mothers are expected to track down the father with the aid of the white county sheriff and make him pay for support. But practically, this is next to impossible. If a father has crossed county lines or fled the state, the sheriff's jurisdiction ends—assuming he was ready to give his time to tracking down the father of a poor and illegitimate Negro baby. Mary Benton is financially a little better off than some chambermaids because she is a graduate of the state's STEP training program, which insures colored scrub-ups a better grade salary. The State Training and Experience Program is operated partially with federal money and it was applied to teach women like Miss Benton how to make beds, clean bathrooms, and what kind of wax to put on floors. All the girls in the program with her were Negroes. The state may have had a menial future in mind for them, to judge from the vocational training. But there was also an educational adjunct to it designed—according to press releases—to complete learning interrupted by poverty and aid in total development. So, during the winter, when cold Atlantic winds whistled down the empty motel corridors on Hilton Head, the ladies went to night courses to qualify for high school diplomas.

"I went regular an' finished it up," she says. "Me an' some other girls carried out all the requirements an' we were supposed to get the diplomas. But that cracker in charge, he never sent 'em."

16

Whatta Ya Mean:
Get a Job?

DESPITE the numbers of poor people in the area and their problems, confirmable by statistics, personal observation, or both, there existed in the summer of 1967 ambivalent feelings in South Carolina about the need for antipoverty efforts. For instance, in the Beaufort county seat of Ridgeland, a white official who had formerly been an Air Force lieutenant colonel, commanding wing, squadron, and group, sat at his desk with a sign on the wall behind him reading:

> Whatta Ya Mean
> Get a Job?
> And Disqualify Myself
> for the Poverty Program?

The man was Ervin Berry, executive director of the Poverty Program. It was officially titled the Jasper-Beaufort County Economic Opportunity Commission.

The commission has been something less than a successful operation. So much less that in July of last year representatives of the poor (black) on its executive and advisory committees sought Mr. Berry's removal, charging, "The poor people have nothing to say about this program. . . . We have seen no significant benefit to the poor as a result of the programs designed and run by the Jasper-Beaufort EOC."

Discord in the Jasper-Beaufort OEC was ordained. The tripartite character of antipoverty organizations (two-thirds Establishment, one-third poor) assures nothing but contention, as the experience of Selma illustrated. Class and racial antagonisms are usually intensified. The dominant two-thirds are willing to dole out a few dollars in order to keep the natives happy and the status quo intact. The natives refuse—for the first time in the nation's history—to be humored or bought off. They have become aware that their title to America is stronger, goes back farther in time than that of most whites. (The *Mayflower* arrived in 1620, but the first black slave had beaten it here by a year.) The status quo, in whatever period of their sojourn, has proved an instrument of oppression and their instinct naturally is to throw off oppression without being concerned whether the status quo survives. They see the Poverty Program as a possible means of changing the very ground rules of their existence, breaking down social and economic barriers, doing battle against the old forces of evil.

But even white men of goodwill included in the two-thirds majority cannot do the job that black wants done. Good white intentions are no substitute for the knowledge that comes from being black and poor. It is a rare man of any color who would consciously undermine a system that insures him physical comfort and boundless prerogatives in order to create real black economic reform. In the unlikely event that such a white paragon appeared on a Dixie poverty board, he would be outvoted by his peers and probably ostracized. Even if he persisted, he would remain a part-time warrior in a battle requiring full-time participation. This would be white representation at its best. At its worst it is the former executive EOC director of another county who was drawing $850 a month while he ran his own business on the side. His secretary cried when Washington investigators arrived unannounced one morning and opened a file to find a monthly work report covering all the time he had lavished on the antipoverty program. The difficulty was that the report had been made out in advance for work allegedly done in the upcoming month. In exchange for his $850 salary, he had been giving ten hours a week.

This kind of behavior has to be expected in anything as

schizophrenic as the Poverty Program, where the federal government supplies the dollars but runs away from control. This is not the normal direction for federal bureaucracy to take and strongly suggests a disinclination for real involvement in implementing the new and controversial idea that the time has come for the poor to make their move out of poverty. In the absence of federal presence, established local powers move in, loving the dollars, despising the idea behind them.

The congressional stamp of approval now has been set on this procedure. The 1967 amendments to the OEO Act in effect give authority over most programs to mayors and other public officials, where once more than 80 percent of control had been in the hands of private groups in acordance with OEO regulations. As bad as many of these groups were, the prospect of Selma Mayor Joe Smitherman and other such officials assuming power over the poor is a grim one. Except in rare cases, they have the authority and expertise to manipulate poverty board composition and to spawn new generations of Happy Pappies, inaugurate more Operation Drainos.

"This racial thing is a real problem," Berry says in his Ridgeland office, where all the clerical help in view is white. "It's trending the other way. But you can't change things overnight. Whites, for example, won't send their kids to the Head Start. They're poor but proud. And, of course, the Negroes around here are a tough lot. I had a good girl working in this office who busted the head of her boy friend the other day. Fifty stitches."

White authority in Jasper-Beaufort decided what groups would be on the dominant two-thirds of the board of directors, always outvoting po' folks. They chose members from such groups as the Jaycee-ettes, the Business and Professional Women's Club, and the Bar Association. The Bar Association had refused to cooperate in a badly needed legal aid program for the poor; following their designation, Jaycee-ettes and professional women visited shack communities with the same frequency as before—never.

As bad as this apportionment was, it would have been worse were it not for the presence of the Penn Community Center. This privately supported institution in the gas-station-and-

general-store town of Frogmore has roots reaching back to the
Civil War, when it began training black generations for careers
and leadership. Rap Brown would find it a poky place hung
up on notions of gentility that can only emasculate black social
and economic revolutionaries; he would be mostly correct. The
Center has the sleepy air of a mission: rambling stucco bunga-
lows, black students walking with mild gait under fatherly oaks
lacy with Spanish moss, a big brass dinner bell bonging to break
the noon quiet. But for all its air of another, more subservient
day, Penn Center has produced graduates who have made an
impact on the Jasper-Beaufort area.

Le Roy Browne was a Penn alumnus elected to the Beaufort
County board of directors, the first elected Negro official in
South Carolina since 1900. Thomas Barnwell is an intense
EOC assistant director who goes into the boondocks on his own
time to involve the historically hapless in their fleeting moment
of opportunity to mean something. There is Mrs. Frieda
Mitchell, still working at Penn and on the EOC board, trying
to find middle ground between her inherent mannerliness and
newfound anger over what she feels is gross mismanagement
of a chance at salvation for her people.

"You can't even get to see proposals," she says. "It's so frustrating. Here you have the federal government giving out all
this money but it's going into the wrong pockets. The ratio of
salaries to programs is ridiculous."

(The closest a visitor without subpoena powers can come to
obtaining a breakdown on money going to staff and recipients
is Mr. Berry's statement that of 425 checks going out each pay-
day from the EOC office, 36 are for office staff, 112 for Head
Start personnel, and the rest for the poor.)

Through the efforts of Penn Center people on the EOC
board, Beaufort got a Head Start program after school officials
had refused to request one. It was a struggle but, as in Baker
County, there was a core of activists to direct it. And if they
had not been there. . . . Even with activist help, the Jasper-
Beaufort EOC is a boy on a man's mission. Application for a
Day Care Center (universally unloved in the South) was batted
around with procedural bumbling and finally denied by the
Atlanta Regional Office when it arrived too late to merit seri-

ous consideration. On-the-job training for adults never made it either, although to find out precisely why would require the services of Philadelphia lawyers versed in the nuances of government statute and Charleston lawyers wise in the ways of interposition.

Eight Head Start schools *were* set up with six hundred children attending. And the first issue of Mr. Berry's community newsletter in the 1967 summer hailed the start of a Roadside Beautification Project for sixty chronically unemployed men:

> This employment will provide a source of income and practical training for a temporary period of time. We firmly believe this training will improve their chances of securing permanent employment in the future.

The program firmly consists of cutting brush and hauling trash.

This insufficiency can't be laid wholly at the feet of Mr. Berry and his EOC. It is part of the underrealized concept and catch-as-catch-can organization of the Poverty Program, nationally and locally. It recalls Gunnar Myrdal's remark that actions under the program are "spurious . . . not carefully planned as the inauguration of a long-term national effort to realize the demands of the national ideal." Roadside Beautification might draw a smile of approval from Mrs. Lyndon Johnson; but it is no substitute for a vast national rehabilitation program altering not just the surface image but the body America, one that makes significant use of unemployed men, who could learn how to lay pipe, for example, while laying it into realms of hookworm, roundworm, and amoeba, and bringing sanitation to Marvin Kenneth in the Rollins' shack.

However, Mr. Berry's list of twenty-seven projects called for "beautifying" historical cemeteries, chamber of commerce road signs, and main highways, where trash receptacles would be placed for use of the "traveling public." But there was not a word about beautifying washboard roads in poor sections or building a park or some decent privies. Instead, Item 24 on the list read:

Clearing right of way and
beautifying road to the
Jasper Country Club

Jasper-Beaufort EOC, like most of its counterparts, is weakest
at what should be a point of strength—liaison with poor people.
That 700-page government catalogue of assistance programs
does no good lying on a desktop. Good can commence only
when the poor and the program to assist them are joined. This
requires numbers of people with time to penetrate into rural
sections where so many of the worst cases reside, ignorant for
the most part that anything is afoot to give them a lift. Their
absence is a critical oversight in the antipoverty tables of organization and once more raises doubts about the validity of
the Washington effort. In Hazard, Kentucky, Mrs. Grigsby was
the only worker going out into a county of 16,000 poor people.
Jasper-Beaufort has three "Neighborhood Workers" *covering
13,000 square miles.*

The time spent tracking down a single case is prohibitive.
One of the workers, Mrs. Harris, lost nearly three hours on a
roasting July afternoon trying to find a young man who had
dropped out of the Youth Corps. First, a twenty-mile drive
from Beaufort into the rural section, then criss-crossing dirt
roads looking for a certain shack, finally finding a young girl
who could locate it, arriving to encounter only an aged aunt
who made a grotesque and fearful curtsy at the sight of Mrs.
Harris' white companion and stammered two or three possible
places the boy might be, the places checked to no avail, and the
expedition ultimately written off as a failure.

Whether or not the boy in such a case will be written off for
good depends on the caliber of the worker and the weight of
other demands on her. Persons conditioned to failure often cannot take the initiative, make the move that might save them.
So a missed connection, a small gap in timing, can produce consequences that might affect a lifetime. Mrs. Harris leaves the
shack, ten minutes later the boy returns, the old aunt tells him
that official people have been there looking for him. She might
even get it straight that it was something about the Youth
Corps. For him to make the twenty miles into Beaufort involves

clearing numerous obstacles, including whatever factors induced him to drop out in the first place. Added to them is the fear that official censure might be waiting, the cost of transportation, the mental and physical imponderables that could beset a teenage boy whom circumstance has placed in an isolated shack with an aging aunt who curtsies before white strangers. So a connection is missed and a tumble into the void begun. Is this an exaggerated image born of the sentimental notion that the poor should be coddled? In a random example like this, with all the details lacking, it could be. It is also easy to be strong and to demand similar strength from that boy, without regard for the abuses he has suffered in a lifetime spent poor and black in the South. Some feel it is incumbent on the society that has acquiesced in the creation of the inveterate poor to make an extraordinary effort to help them.

It isn't easy. Assistant EOC Director Robert Barnwell feels the effort should be made and moves on his own time to make it. Perhaps it is easier for him or, at least, more urgent because he is black. The same afternoon that Mrs. Harris tried unsuccessfully to find her young "case," he drove out after work to another shack where an old black couple live with their daughter and her four children. The old man owns a few acres; they have a sow, bearing fig trees, a good garden, and a habitable shack. But the children are raggedy; money is being spent on food that could go for clothes if the family would enroll in the Beaufort County food stamp program. Barnwell tries to explain to the daughter that by buying a few dollars' worth of stamps they could save $40 or $50 a month on food bills. She sits listening, fat and suspicious, her surest knowledge of white largesse to black the $20 a week she earns as a domestic. Her hair is up in pin curlers under a turban, and indignation crackles in the air around her head.

"I don't know," she tells Barnwell. "My mind isn't with it. If they want to give us somethin', why don't they put it in a check? I'm a funny person. I don't like to ask people for things. People may do them but they don't like it."

"You wouldn't be asking for anything," Barnwell replies. "It's a right. We worked hard to make these crackers give us this right to government food. But it's even harder when you finally get the door open and people like you won't walk in."

"All right, Martin Luther King," she answers, and smiles.

Nothing is decided by the time Barnwell drives off. On top of his car is a screen door he has made for a shack family living near his home and he will deliver it before returning to *his* family. There are not many Barnwells in this world.

And even he has been unable to help Donald Chestnut. Chestnut is black, eighty-four years old and earns his living plowing behind his horse for hire at $6 a day. He lives near Frogmore with his wife in a decrepit shack. They have been unable to get a dime out of South Carolina welfare despite efforts by people in the EOC. The sticking point, apparently, is that he owns five acres of land, and welfare had said he must divest himself of these properties before he could receive old-age benefits. So, desirous of keeping his land, Chestnut hitches up his seventeen-year-old horse and goes out plowing.

"All I do in my life is farmin'," he says, a smile displaying a mouthful of stained and splintered stumps of teeth. "We used to have thirty acres but that got away from us. Now on the five I got I planted an acre of tomatoes an' an acre of corn. But the corn didn't come. Squirrels got it. Tomatoes come good, yeah. My old woman's puttin' some up."

In the yard under a wild locust tree, his wife filled Mason jars with stewed tomatoes swimming in a galvanized wash-bucket, watermelon rinds sweetening the brew. She is a bare-foot, pig-tailed relic of another time, too old to remember her "white" manners.

"Do we have runnin' water?" she says, deadpan. "Yeah. Run-nin' outa that pump yonder. What's that old man over there tellin' you? He don't know. Maybe we can't be able to eat directly. I can't tell. Only one Man I know knows that. The only One I can trust."

Mr. Chestnut's memory slides in and out of the present. The farm "got away" in 1975. His wife was born in 1928. But after he gets used to the unexpected visit, he gathers his mind together and speaks carefully.

"In 1956 I paid a two-hundred-dollar hospital bill. Deposit, that's right, it was seventy-five dollars deposit to get in. I pay my own bills but I know I'm entitled to get 'em paid, old as I am. But they ain't gonna do it. They desire me to give up my acres which *I* ain't gonna do. I got some tater plants, peas, an' some peanuts. I need to keep them. What zactly do they tell me at welfare? Truth is, I forget. It's been so long. But while that horse holds out—he's still a good horse—I take care of myself an' that woman. She still have to work the fields sometime an' she done eighty. Still ain't done eighty-one, though."

It sounded like a sentence.

17

Sometimes Dropouts Drop Out

JOHN GADSON—a self-assured and hardworking Penn Center alumnus—is director of the Neighborhood Youth Corps, heart of the Jasper-Beaufort antipoverty campaign. During the summer of 1967, 325 high school students from poor families made about $30 a week in a variety of temporary jobs scraped together over both counties. The jobs enabled the students to contribute to their families, buy clothing for school, and have some fun. While it did not come close to reaching everyone eligible, the program pushed through by Gadson was a creditable and encouraging development.

But the record on the dropout side of the program is not so bright. They are the youth most needful, since their link to an education that might lead them off the poverty treadmill has been broken. Gadson had only one hundred openings for three hundred applicants (with perhaps another three hundred potential applicants out there in the shacks, never heard from). The pay rate was $1.25 an hour, with work limited to three eight-hour days. Enrollees also were required to attend night classes leading to a high school diploma. On paper, it was all very promising; in practice, the promise is hard to deliver.

"The job market is just about closed in this area," Gadson says. "What this means is—"

The phone rings and after listening a minute he says:

"Betty, all the jobs we had for girls are placed. It doesn't look too good right now. But I'll tell them how much you want to work and we'll put your name up top of the list. All right, honey? Fine. We won't forget."

Gadson picks up his conversation without reference to the call.

"With jobs so scarce, if we didn't have Parris Island we'd really be in trouble. I'll say they've given good cooperation. But generally here there's an overconcern about too much money being spent on Negroes, a constant effort to soft-pedal the fact that the Poverty Program *is* mostly about Negroes.

"Still, we've had some successes. Girls working at the base hospital as ward attendants, in the laundry room, learning hospital routine. A few even have gotten on civil service lists. The boys are getting some mechanics, meat cutting, carpentry. Part of the problem we have is teaching them the disciplined attitudes of a workingman in place of the lax way they've been drifting. I understand the sociological reasons but they still have to shape up. The problem is, the salary we can pay is so low it's hard to compete with seasonal day labor on a farm or the packing house in the fall, where they can get eighty dollars a week. Of course, it's only for a couple of months and there's absolutely no future. But it's money in the pocket. So the dropouts from school drop out from us."

The basic education program, the same kind of wise and humanistic touch that enabled Mr. Dawkins to solve the puzzle of Jo-Jo, functions out of two centers where the dropouts are expected to go for classes for two hours, two nights a week. They can and do live anywhere within the 13,000 square miles of Jasper-Beaufort, and the transportation problem often is acute, particularly among young people with a built-in low incentive toward book learning. No provision is made in the program for transportation. They say that Abraham Lincoln, in the early part of the nineteenth century, walked five or ten miles to school. Perhaps he would walk it today. Or, more likely —given his political character—he would be organizing protests because the classes that teenage dropouts are supposed to attend are also used by adult whites and Negroes enrolled in Basic Adult Education. The curriculum usually sails above the heads of the dropouts, and their sketchy attendance reflects it.[100] Five or six have gone off to the Job Corps in distant training centers, where they received $25 a month allowance, banked $50 and reported to Gadson that they were making progress. But others who entered the Rural Job Corps quickly returned home. No matter how you slice it, they said, cutting brush is cutting brush. Back home, there was more optimism.

"I used to spend my days mostly walkin' aroun', lookin' for somethin'," says Herbert Purvis, nineteen, who completed tenth grade, dropped out, and now has dropped in to Gadson's program. "Best you could find was gas station or somethin' at six dollars a day. Now I help an air-conditionin' man at PI [Parris Island]. He treats me pretty good, don't ride hog on me. I can't say I know how to repair one yet but I just about know how to see what's wrong. If I could stick with this I could see somethin' ahead. But if it don't last, I don't know, that's somethin' different."

Douglas Johnson, seventeen, was a B student when he quit in the ninth grade in 1963 to help his mother. She has eleven children, a departed husband, and makes $20 a week as a domestic. Johnson still is kiddish, his eyes on the verge of a smile as he tries to discuss himself seriously, breaking into a grin and self-deprecating shrug at weightier questions about his hopes for the future.

"I was workin' in the packin' house durin' last season," he says. "But if I'd of gone back there this year then I would've been out when they shut down again. This way I might get somethin' regular someday. Out at PI I do carpenter work—help 'em hold things, drive nails. Suh? Makin progress? Yes, suh. I give my mama fifteen dollars a week an' I bought myself a pair of boots. It's worthwhile."

Dora Williams, twenty, dropped out of high school in 1965, when she became pregnant. She stayed home a year with the baby but there were six brothers and sisters at home for her mother to support and she joined the Youth Corps. It brought a clerical job at PI, where she typed and filed. She wears a fresh, bright dress, her hair is neatly pulled back in a bun, and her gaze is steady and alert.

"I learned a lot at PI," she says. "And I'm going to get my diploma at the night classes. Yes, definitely. Then there are civil service tests coming up I want to take. I think maybe a company around here would hire a Negro girl. None have but I think they might."

Purvis, Johnson, and Miss Williams are not success stories yet. But they have a chance to make it in the system's nine-to-five world where, like it or not, the material ground for most lives is laid. Their position is precarious; they know friends who could not enter the job program because it was filled and others who dropped out; they are impatient with $30-a-week earnings and realize that in the absence of any governmental effort to "induce labor" their training may be a rehearsal for a show that never opens. They live with race as a job qualification. But, for the first time, they perceive a way that does not lead to a motel job on Hilton Head. They know about the sign— Whatta Ya Mean, Get a Job? But even to put it down with a kid's sarcastic thrust is clearly beneath them.

18

On the Shrimp Docks One Morning

HILTON HEAD ISLAND once—not so long ago—was all black. It was connected to the mainland by ferry and the Negro community farmed and fished, mostly as tenants for absentee white owners of farms and shrimp boats. Then, in the early 1950's, two Northerners who owned most of the good land decided to exploit its tourist potential. Motels rose on fine beaches and golf greens sprouted on the dunes. The state, which never had been able to build a bridge to the mainland for black residents, erected one for the tourists in 1958. It could be argued— and is—that white development brought economic betterment to black chambermaids and to a generation of career caddies. However, a chambermaid-caddy economy never made anyone except motel owners solvent. There were on Hilton Head two or three Negro fishermen who had scrimped over the years and cajoled loans or credit, and had been able to buy boats of their own and turn a narrow profit margin. For the rest, the community was about as poor and shacky as any on the South Carolina mainland.

Civil rights activity, combined with the advent of the Poverty Program, raised black hopes on Hilton Head and today some of those hopes are painstakingly being realized. FHA loans have been obtained to purchase six shrimp boats and two crabbers; never mind the years they had not been obtained, at last it is being accomplished and the surface fact of the loans seems impressive. Foundation of a shrimp cooperative is bruited about, with federal government money behind it. A moving force in these ventures is David Jones, forty, a tall, husky, and studious man who lives with his family in one of the best Negro houses on Hilton Head. The house is modest by any measure, a small frame dwelling of six rooms with a neat flower garden in front and beside it a cinder-block garage.

Jones has achieved this black affluence because he is a one-man band of industriousness—he is an auto mechanic, a preacher, a motel janitor, a shrimp boat operator, chairman of the proposed shrimp co-op, and one of three Negroes elected to Beaufort County's nine-man Board of Directors. At ten o'clock this evening, he is still in his small office after a day that began at dawn, filling out FHA applications for another fisherman who would like to buy a shrimp boat. He is a moral man with a sense of duty who concedes he had a better break than most black men around him. His father, who ran the first ferry from the island to the mainland, was also a top chef and made good money. So the son was able to go to Penn Center and then on to North Carolina Agriculture and Technical College, when most of the young men in his immediate generation were already trudging down dead-end roads.

In 1960, Jones obtained one of the then-rare (and still remarkable) FHA loans to expand his auto repair garage. Not to refurbish it, which would have meant the kind of sizable loan that whites obtain as a matter of course. This merely extended the shell. You can walk off the size of the loan, starting where the old, dark cinder block ends and a lighter shade begins. You walk about fifteen feet to the end of the loan.[101] Inside there is room for one car but no grease pit. A car under repair is propped up on jacks, blocks, and oil drums like a combination of Rube Goldberg and Gasoline Alley.

"The Poverty Program hasn't done anything on Hilton Head," he says in a mellifluous voice with Jamaican overtones. "Except the loans. And that's something we should have been getting all along. Why not? People here tried to set up poverty committees to say what should be done but they never had a chance. No one listened, nothing happened. The women without husbands and lots of kids, the old people, they really need help but it never comes to them.

"Last year I finally got an FHA to buy my shrimp boat and we have others that may be coming through on top of what we have. There *is* a Negro FHA agent in this county,[102] something unusual. Now we're trying to get an FHA loan for the shrimp co-op. Thirty thousand dollars so we can put up an icehouse, buy a two-ton to haul, build a little railway to pull our boats from the water. Today we have to pay five dollars each box to have it packed and iced. We eliminate that, truck it to the best market we can find, instead of the local ones who pay what they want, and maybe we can start seeing some money. We applied for the co-op fourteen months ago. Two months ago we heard it passed and then it didn't. Now we don't know."

Shrimp boating is surrounded by an aura of glamour, partly traceable to the song about the shrimp boats coming with their sails in sight, the hurry-up signal for dancing tonight. It is not all that romantic, nowadays at least. The most that an individual black captain grosses in a year is $5,000 to $6,000. His mate gets a third, his expenses come out, and what is left could fit comfortably into a shrimp cocktail cup.

"Go down to the docks tomorrow morning," Jones says, "and see how it is."

At dawn, colorful arrow signs along the road invite the tourist: Come See the Shrimp Boats.

The docks are not picturesque, merely worn shabby by age and sea air alongside a glassy inlet where a humid morning breeze carries the taste of salt. Most of the boats have already left on a dark tide; the few anchored in the inlet are stubby, high-bowed, with booms resting upright that at sea swing out to raise the nets. Orange hemp tassels hanging from the nets brighten the clamshell gray of the docks. One boat with a rusted and pitted rudder has been pulled onto an improvised dry dock and two black men are working under the hull. A piny white patch of new board is bright beside the old ones with their peeled chimney-red paint and stubble of barnacles. One of the men is stuffing cotton into cracks between the boards and the other is daubing the bottom with fresh red paint. He is Walter Greene, about fifty, ten years older than the boat he has just purchased with an FHA loan of $4,000.

To the landlubber knowing little about shrimp boats, it doesn't look like much. Not even sails grace the forty-year-old tub with a rusted rudder and a leaky bottom. No one could accuse the FHA, after years of parsimony with black applicants, of suddenly turning spendthrift. But this appraisal, correct as it might or might not be, does not allow for the opinion of the man under the boat, who owned her—Walter Greene, who was painting *his* boat.

"I worked boats from here to Key West," he says, disregarding a fat coastal mosquito on his nose. "John, stick some more cotton up there by the joinin'. I was mate for twenty-five years. Took a third. That figures to thirty, thirty-five dollars a week in a decent season. You have to follow the shrimp, be away from home. It's hardly no life, for the money as a mate. With three kids you put nothin' by an' scarcely tread water.

"All those years I wanted a boat but I never could've had it until this FHA. Sure couldn't." His brush bled the red into the cotton, laying down next a thick swab of it to help bind the seam. "Then I just got it bought an' it sprung a leak on the starboard side. You see here. But it ain't bad. The boat was rebuilt ten years ago an' the engine runs pretty good. We'll have it ready pretty quick now."

After chasing shrimp on other men's boats from Hilton Head to Key West and beyond during twenty-five years, Greene did not elaborate on how it felt to own. He had reached a certain age when enthusiasms are blunted, dreams arrive too late. But the appreciation of need still drew a quick pulse.

"I knows of two or three others tryin' to get the FHA," he says. "Virgil Orange, for one. He got eleven head of children an' surely needs it. He works as a mate, same as I did. He plants a garden but he ain't able to stay home to farm right. I know. With food an' things high as they is, if you just sit down an' study you don't know *how* he makes it hisself. There's a lot of people, you can't figure how they do it. How you did it yourself. You got to live pretty stingy, that's all."

His brush continues slapping paint onto what is finally his after how many voyages for how many other captains on how many mornings like this he cannot remember. What he feels painting that hull must necessarily include the sum of all those tides that carried him out and returned him after each brimming catch to live pretty stingy on shore. He must also know how Virgil Orange feels as he waits for somebody to decide whether the government of the United States of America has $4,000 to spare, loan on interest, for him; Walter Greene is one of a handful of men in the world who knows exactly how Orange feels. Watch him on the shrimp dock one morning, think of the acres of seas he has crossed to arrive where he is, think where he has come from and where Orange and his children are, and where they may go without the loan. It is hard to imagine how the government of the United States of America can afford not to spare it.

19

Whatever Happened to Merry Maria?

DRIVING U.S. 1 into the city of Pompano on the Florida Atlantic Coast is a dazzling experience. The sun strikes off the sea, sand glistens, and tall motels and hotels white as bleached clamshells gleam along the highway like reflectors. The buildings, stretching mile after effulgent mile, dressed at their bases with palms and mint-green lawns, their balconies open to sea breezes under a washed-blue sky, are a vision of Babylonian luxury, an architectural invitation to the traveler to stop and partake of the creamy joys that the good life has to offer.

Five minutes' drive inland from the Pompano beaches is the Pompano Farm Labor Camp. There are one hundred and fifty two-family wooden buildings consisting of two rooms each, no toilets, and no baths. These are the homes of migrant and local farm workers. It is a better-than-average camp compared to others, north and south; it is also a desolate, dilapidated compound where migrant poverty is shut out of common sight and so does not disturb tourists whose morning orange, afternoon salad, and evening celery may have been picked by the people living there.

The camp was built in a sandy wasteland by the federal government before World War II as emergency farm housing. That was more than twenty-five years ago. In a quarter century, no effort was made to landscape the camp, to set out trees for shade and beauty, or plant grass where children could play.

Today the sand is littered with bottles and other trash, pocked with stagnant puddles, and peopled with Negroes, Puerto Ricans, and Mexicans. Rock, soul music, and a Latin American cacophony blare from shack radios. From time to time, figures move across the sand toward a long shed with small cinder-block structures at either end. These are the communal bath-rooms and wash sheds, each unit serving the long rows of dwell-ings on the four blocks that make up the perimeter of the field. In the men's and women's bathrooms, serving about two hun-dred persons each, there are no doors on the six commode stalls and no seats on the commodes. An inch of water from leaking pipes is collected in sections of the sloping cement floor. Faucets are missing from half a dozen sinks; there is no hot water in the sinks or in the three shower stalls. On one wall of the wom-en's bathroom, someone has signed herself Merry Maria in a childish lipsticked scrawl.

Outside under the shed are two rows of metal wash tubs. They are not being used this July morning but water sprays continuously from sprung pipes and the floor is awash. The houses, bathrooms, and sinks are owned by the Pompano Hous-ing Authority, which took them over from the federal govern-ment. The Authority has long been dominated by the growers of Broward County, who often pay the $4 a month rental for a family, which is not so much a generous gesture as an assertion of control over the worker in the field who is indebted and in debt for his living quarters. There are 15,000 migrant workers in Broward, part of the 100,000 worker force in Florida, which counts agriculture as its number one industry.[103] Nearly 80 percent of the migrants are black, 15 percent are Latin Americans, and the remainder white Americans. Their families are inevitably large and it is common for eight or ten persons to live in the two rooms of each unit. Some families have boarded up an 8 by 8 outside porch to make a third room. Camp maintenance foreman John Hammer, a Negro who still looks strong as a bull at seventy-seven, has seen a lifetime of coming and going at the camp.

"I came here to work when they built it in 1939," he says. "Conditions here are a way off from what they were then. Gone down steadily, that's the story. I try to keep it up but it's past keeping up. There's no money here now. Years ago camp people could make a living on the bean farms in Broward during the winter. The places where you see those fine buildings and motels all used to be beans. You still got the people but you don't have the land. The cost of living goes up but the wages don't for what work there is. People just have to scratch."

The current plight of migrants and the conditions under which they have historically existed is a well-known story in a country with a remarkable tolerance for such stories of deprivation. The so-called Eastern Migrant Stream that sluggishly rolls north over harvest beds from the Carolinas to Connecticut is as predictable as the Gulf Stream. But while numerous government agencies concern themselves with the Gulf Stream, its effect on the ecology of the sea, on weather and icebergs, the flow of the migrants elicits little or no concern. Their itinerant existence renders them even more vulnerable than black tenant farmers; under unwritten laws of exploitation of human beings for profit, every level of government north and south has acceded to their degradation and even encouraged it. Unable to meet residency requirements because of their nomadism, they do not receive the scraps some politicians throw to the stationary poor in exchange for a vote. The health and education of children called into the fields at seven and eight is disregarded by authority with an indifference that would be callous were they the offspring of some hostile alien band in the nation's midst. Enlightened communities that have ASPCA committees for the protection of dumb animals permit migrants to live at barely human levels, whether they are back in their Florida "homes" like the Pompano camp or in Northern quarters.

During July in Pompano, a majority of the camp is on the road and living in generally worse conditions up north. Farmers there have them only for a brief month or two and accordingly try to squeeze out the most work for the least expenditure during that time. Since I first became a reporter in New York fifteen years ago, not a year has gone by without one newspaper in the metropolitan area "exposing" migrant living conditions with fulminating editorials and scant effect. Last summer was no exception. The New York *Times,* for example,

concentrated on New Jersey, where an estimated 15,000 Negro
migratory workers arrive each summer in broken-down trucks
and ramshackle buses. They are herded along by black crew
leaders whose role of bartering men for profit is reminiscent
of Angolan slave traders of centuries past. The *Times* sent reporters into a number of the state's 1,100 migrant camps, some
of which New Jersey Governor Richard J. Hughes conceded
were "inhuman."

Here is a description of the end of the trail from Pompano
as reported by the *Times:*

> At one farm in Vineland, Negroes have been crowded into
> chicken coops. In another, they cook, drink and bathe from a
> foul water tap that has been grossly polluted by a nearby privy
> that has overflown [*sic*]. In every camp, flies swarm over the gar-
> bage-strewn dust, the young children and the cooking grits and
> stolen vegetables that migrants usually live on.
>
> At night in the camps as many as six or more children are
> stacked like cordwood onto one roach-infested bed. When hordes
> of mosquitoes take over from the flies, it is the time when sullen
> men drink cheap wine called 'Tiger Rose' that they bought for a
> dollar a bottle from their Negro crew leaders who paid 50 cents
> for it.
>
> Many children have distended navels, indicating malnutrition,
> and many also were ridden with lice and ticks. Worm-infested
> infants, left unattended in the camps for hours by their mothers
> in the fields, are sometimes bitten by rats.

There was a time when a journalistic exposé of women laboring in sweatshops or children forced to work when they should
play aroused the American conscience to remedial action. The
fact that the migrants are either black or Latins contributes to
the present public indifference; but consciences in a surfeited
society are swollen, sluggish. Governor Hughes appointed a
Migrant Labor Task Force, but it was thwarted by the powerful
influence of the New Jersey Farm Bureau and an infinite patience on the part of state officials, who waited for farmers to
improve conditions voluntarily.[104] After the State Migrant Labor Bureau approved one farm which the task force had found
"rife" with violations of the bureau's own code, task force
member Mrs. Lora Liss threatened to resign, saying:

"If these squalid camps can pass a state inspection, then we must stop the state from recruiting Southern Negroes to come here and live in them."

Still, the seasonal shuttling of tens of thousands of people between nothing in the South and less in the North goes on without hindrance. The numbers are reduced only by mechanization—machines that pick tomatoes and are learning to pick oranges—and the spillover of migrants into the cul-de-sac of Northern ghettos where welfare for the untrained and illiterate becomes a way of life for most, riot a release for some, and urban disabusement of the rural dream that life turns good in the city the experience of all. Those who return south after months of labor in the "stream" come home broke or near broke. The system, with its gouges for transportation and "company store" food, for Tiger Rose and social security deductions exacted by farmers but rarely paid into the Social Security Administration, is designed to keep them broke. Crew leaders, farm owners, and state officials desirous of keeping Farm Bureaus happy know that the economic vulnerability of the migrant is a guarantee of a ready pool of needy flesh when the next year's crop is ready for picking.

This is the migrant cycle. Farmers say that it must be maintained if America is to eat. Critics believe that no system that debases people should persist, that the cycle must be broken since the system has proved itself incapable of reform. To get the crops in, they argue, is the farmers' problem and one that can be solved by the determined, albeit costly, application of technology. To get the people out is more difficult. In Pompano during the last two years, the Poverty Program has created the hope that the Migrant Stream can be dammed. It is a small hope, but it is the first the migrants have ever had, the first time they have been offered anything but a dollar bill at the end of a bean row. For children previously condemned by circumstance to drift in the stream toward personal unfulfillment and social inconsequence, there may be salvation, even, perhaps, for Merry Maria, whoever she was, wherever she went after her young exuberance moved her to proclaim her identity on the wall of the women's communal bathroom of the Pompano Labor Camp. I pictured her with sunny brown eyes and long black hair, a nondescript skirt and blouse graced by an eager and guileless body, a slender olive arm reaching up with a lipstick to inscribe herself on the unmerry wall. If time has not already done too much to her, there could be a chance at salvation for Maria.

20

Salvation in a Small Place

THE Community Action office of the Florida Migrant Program operates out of a Pompano store about twenty feet wide. It is supposed to help service some 14,000 migrant poor in Broward County in addition to coordinating work in other counties. The Broward numbers alone suggest a full-strength Army division; the problem faced in the summer of 1967 by OEO Regional Director William Johnson (since promoted to state project director) is how to run a division-size campaign from headquarters no bigger than a company orderly room and with company-size resources.

"They call this a war on poverty," he says. "But what kind of war is this when most people don't really want you to win?"

The question is appropriate from Johnson, a black man in his mid-thirties who has been in action a long while. Johnson comes from the Migrant Stream. When he was thirteen he plowed behind a mule for $1.25 a day, never seeing the inside of a school during harvest time, when they closed to permit schoolchildren to quit desks for bean rows. Crop priority over education is an old and sometimes unavoidable rural story that has condemned generations of black and white children to ignorance. Johnson escaped, narrowly, from becoming just another victim of "agribusiness." A white judge who devoted his life to helping migrant children liberated him.

"Broward County Juvenile Department Judge Don Davis," Johnson says. "I worship that man. He saved me."

Judge Davis supplied encouragement, counsel, and money, and anonymous donors eventually enabled Johnson to get out from behind the mule and into Morehouse College in Atlanta. He is grateful but not beholden. He has seen too many men like himself wrecked by the system ever again to be on easy terms with a society that tolerates it.

"The migrant cycle has got to be broken," Johnson declares. "It is murdering people, those who stay in it and those who slip out. Go into any Northern slum and find out where most of the people came from. They came from the rural South. From places like the Pompano camp. It's bad enough but not nearly the worst. Local sanitarians are supposed to inspect farm camps. They don't. The Labor Department *could* exert its inspection authority here but it doesn't. We've had a request in for two years to the Department of Agriculture and to Housing and Urban Development to replace the shacks. Nothing is done. If people in the camps complain as individuals, the Man says, 'If you don't like the place, get the hell out.' Now with the OEO for the first time there is an organization to carry the ball for the poor and there is some hope." [105]

A variety of programs peck away at migrant needs. In 1966, OEO allocated $610,000 to run Youth Corps programs in *fourteen* Florida counties with heaviest migrant populations. Last year the appropriation was cut to $434,000, providing places for 333 youngsters in a region with well over a hundred thousand migrants. The Labor Department's Manpower Development and Training Program moved into six counties during 1967 with admirable plans to train heads of households for jobs as cooks, engine repairmen, and communications technicians. But there was room only for about five hundred persons. The Florida State Education Department was given $1,249,000 last year to operate Adult Summer Vocational courses for migrants throughout the state.

"Basically," says Johnson, "it's a good program. Especially since part of the idea is to keep families off the road. Keep a family together with a little money to live on instead of following that dead-end trail north. Heads of families received thirty dollars a week and three dollars for each dependent for going back to school, with the men given vocational training in addition to writing and arithmetic, and the women taught sewing or home nursing. But in all of Florida there were only fifteen hundred openings with one hundred and seventy-one here in Broward. We received three hundred and twelve applications but even that figure is misleading. Thousands need and would want such programs but they don't know about them. And with all the need and wanting, do you know that Florida turned back four hundred thousand of the original one million, two hundred and forty-nine thousand dollars? Couldn't find people to spend it on."

In the fragmented world of the Poverty Program, it is not surprising that each of the three major migrant programs—Youth Corps, Manpower Training, and Adult Education—is administered by a separate agency, thereby producing partial and piecemeal efforts to solve interlocking migrant problems. Given the history of OEO, neither is it surprising that William Johnson, whose expertise in such problems began from the ground up behind a plow, was relegated to running a counseling service when he might profitably have been fashioning and implementing programs to have an immediate effect on the drifting lives around him. But Johnson's basic function was to see that his staff—thirty-three persons to cover fourteen counties—dispensed advice and whatever extracurricular service they could squeeze in. Thirty-three workers to inform one hundred thousand migrants about housing and sanitation, educational opportunities, home management, legal rights. . . .

Success is measured in individual stories about children persuaded to stay in school instead of dropping out, an old man who learned to put money in a savings account, a Puerto Rican family successfully counseled on how to get an FHA loan so that one transcendent day they moved from their shack into a neat house with a bathroom and terrazzo floors. There is the nineteen-year-old boy who knew only how to cut sugarcane until put in contact with the Youth Corps, where he learned welding, became more proficient than his teacher, and now is making the kind of money that can bring order and decency into a life. There is the sixteen-year-old girl whom one of Johnson's staff sent to work in a white woman's house. The girl did not know how to vacuum because she had never seen a vacuum cleaner, did not understand window washing because her shack had no windows. She learned the rudiments of housekeeping, and while Johnson decries the notion that her salvation should be a life sentence as a domestic, he sees interim benefits from her labors during the transitional period from shack to a more stable place in the social order.

"The world of work outside a bean row for the migrant child is a thing apart," he maintains. "If he or she learns to be on time, to be responsible, to handle money, maybe to save—something at least has begun. In the Youth Corps, for example, they get thirty-seven dollars a week. Most of them have never *seen* thirty-seven dollars at one time before. If they absorb lessons in discipline, working together, how to dress, then the job is a partial success. Even if they learn no skill, an element of hope has been implanted that life holds something better. Ultimately, it's only through education and vocational training they can ever break out and start supporting families like the rest of America is accustomed to. The trouble is, these programs already are in jeopardy, snatching back a hope as they give it. If they don't keep the admittedly inadequate programs in existence, even those few people in them will be thrown to the wolves."

The wolves almost got Mae-Troy Blakely, and she isn't sure exactly how she got away. She's thirty-one now, her plump, dark face serious, her hands carefully manicured. Those hands were pulling potatoes from a North Carolina field when she was five or six, working along with half a dozen brothers and sisters. In a family rendered destitute by a father who drank and a mother's chronic illness, Miss Blakely made it through the junior year of high school. Six years ago, she picked her last row, "moving up" to domestic work. Johnson hired her in 1966 (most of his aides are former migrants) and last year she was chosen to attend a course in community development at the University of Wisconsin. This is the kind of miracle OEO at its best can work, and she tells of it with ingenuous pride.

"I don't know what made me want a better way," she says, driving her 1960 Chevvy on a medical run. "It was just in me. When I got the chance to go to the university, my mother cried.

I remember she said, 'It looks like you're gonna make it, Mae-Troy.' "

Miss Blakely's style as an OEO worker recalls Mrs. Grigsby in Kentucky or Thomas Barnwell in South Carolina. All three are motivated beyond the limits of their job description; they are *of* the people needing their help and their blood knowledge of those needs transforms duty into concern. The Poverty Program could exploit their kind of involvement on a mass scale (if it had the money, if it had the vision) to reach knowledgeable, compassionate hands into all the dark corners of American poverty.

Miss Blakely's work this day is the kind that only a former migrant could do, week in, week out, the frustrating and sometimes exasperating work of helping the hapless to help themselves without losing patience or initiative when efforts at self-help seem minimal. She is going to round up people who need to go to the doctor but deep down fight against going. She can do it because she understands the crippling psychological effect of ignorance and poverty on energy and character; she knows what it is to limp.

"Now first we're going to pick up a Mexican lady that has to be carried to the doctor," she says. "The appointment is for twelve-thirty and it's twelve-twenty now. But she won't be ready. When you tell them twelve-thirty they start getting *ready* at twelve-thirty even if you explain that they have to be ready to *be* there at twelve-thirty."

Outside a shack resounding with cha-cha music she blows the horn and calls out for the woman. Children pop from the building, scurry back. A young man says that his mother is not ready. She will be ready soon. All right, Miss Blakely says.

This is a medical run, which may not come under any specific subtitle of poverty legislation but is prominent under the Pompano office's unofficial heading of Jobs That Have to Get Done to Help Poor Sick People. There is a Cuban family in the next shack that has made its own renewal effort: a simple white picket fence surrounds a mini-garden where sunflowers and pansies brighten the sandy soil. A two-year-old child has been passing blood. His father comes to the car, a slight man with a slender black moustache. He greets Miss Blakely respectfully in his small English and explains that the boy isn't ready yet. Can he be ready in fifteen minutes? Maybe. She will be back then. Maybe he could go tomorrow? No. Today. It is very necessary to see the doctor today. All right, he will try.

"You see, that father, he's just not used to doing things in the orderly way our society expects," she says, already searching for another house. "Going to a doctor is something rare, a big event. They're afraid of it and, you know, they'd sooner not face up to it. Now something else. You take a man like him and get him to start in the education and training program. If there happened to be room, which there isn't. It's just hard to keep him going, to make him see that it might lead to something. Quite a few have refused to go because they were ashamed of not being able to read or write. Then, you take a man who's done farming all his life, that's the only thing he knows, the only place where he's sure of himself. So if he does somehow get through the program and maybe learns a skill, I'm afraid that without a determined follow-up he'll just slip right back. All it takes is one or two turndowns for a job. They're just so sensitive to discouragement they quit on themselves. But we don't hardly have the money or people to program him, no less follow him up."

She spots the place of Jenny Moore, where there is a legal problem that Director Johnson is working on and she stops for a minute. Mrs. Moore is a widow with eight children living in two rooms on $85 a month welfare, which she augments by picking with some of the children during the local season. A seventeen-year-old son who left home to find work got a ride on the road from some boys who, she says, took him along on a robbery. Her son was sentenced as a first offender to *six months to twenty years;* it seems incredible on the face of it so Johnson is trying to establish the elusive, precise facts. Mrs. Moore is tall, willowy, her hands still surprisingly supple. But her nerves are gone. She speaks in a rapid-fire whine, stutters, folds and unfolds her hands, rolls her eyes. A daughter, Lucy Lois, comes from behind a shower curtain used as a room divider and gives the visitors water to drink from Mason jars. Lucy Lois looks like her mother and, like her mother, works in the fields, picking beans on weekends, when she is not attending seventh-grade classes—and sometimes during the week when money runs out. Both mother and daughter are suffering from some kind of eye trouble; the emotional relationship between them is close and suggests a psychosomatic cause; both have the same nervous grace in their hands.

"I have all the—the responsibility on me," the mother says. "And my—m-m-my mind's on my son. See her eye? Rr-rr-runny all the time. Each day my eye it—it gets w-w-worser an' worser, w-w-weaker an' w—weaker. Wind blew sand one—one day. Trash got in it. I don't—I don't know what's gonna happen. By the t-t—time I pays rent an' lights, buy—buy the children a p-p—piece or two. Look at me. I'm dr—dryin' up an' gettin' ugly. But—but s-s—some day soon God will o—open things up."

In the car, Miss Blakely voices her awareness of Mrs. Moore's psychological difficulties but there is no agency available to minister to the mind of a migrant's widow. Should a day come when the stammering mind falters, there will be seven children left to face some mental and physical problems of their own. The eighth has the temporary sanctuary of jail. While Director Johnson tries to ascertain the facts of the case he is also trying to find funds for legal services for people who cannot afford lawyers. The law, for them, holds the same terrors as disease. But the luxury of legal aid is part of the fat that congressmen denounce in the Poverty Program, fat that is being trimmed with meat-ax efficiency.

Miss Blakely retraces her route and now the Cuban child is ready along with his mother and two sisters, dressed in Sunday clothes, their black hair glossy, faces grave and silent; the Mexican grandmother hobbles out; a middle-aged Negro woman in a bandana completes the group. But the doctor's office is closed when they arrive; a woman who has been waiting for an hour says he never showed up.

"The last doctor we had here was good," Miss Blakely says. "But this one, you never know."

She waits fifteen minutes, half an hour. The baby is restless, the older women confused and apprehensive. She will take them home and try to find out why the doctor has not come and she will arrange to have him there later in the day. Can they be ready if she comes by later? Their faces are vague; they

think so, probably. But they clearly have their doubts and sus-
picions. Miss Blakely tries to reassure them. Her manner says:
What seems impossible now is only difficult. Depend on me.
You can trust me to make the day happen correctly.

She is downcast after the last passenger leaves; it has taken
much persuasion and arranging to set up the appointments,
and with their small tolerance for discouragement there is no
guarantee she can produce the patients once she gets the doctor
pinned down. A child waves and she stops. There is a Puerto
Rican lady, the child's mother, whom she has not seen in a
while. Confessora Rodriguez has been in the United States for
eleven years and the essentials of her life have not changed
much since she left a small farm outside San Juan. Is life better
here than there?

"*Todo depende,*" she says—it all depends. It is the noncom-
mittal Latin answer to questions that lead to no clear, fixed
response. Does her husband earn enough working in the fields?

"*Cuando se encuentra,*" she says—when he finds it.

He had gone north but could not tolerate the conditions
there and worried about the family when he was away. The
children—two barefoot boys and a little girl with thin, small
golden earrings—are gay and beautiful. They live on rice and
beans, the mother says, but their dark eyes seem radiant with
health.

"*No tenemos carne ninguna,*" she declares emphatically.
"*Aqui, sufrimos mucho.*"

Miss Blakely corroborates her words in the car.

"Families like that rarely if ever see meat," she says. "And
they do suffer, yes. The children are strong now because they're
so young. But it catches up with them. Her husband is working
around here now at a dollar twenty an hour. He can't provide
and he knows it. But as long as there's some work at a dollar
twenty an hour, he doesn't want to leave it go for a training
program that gives him thirty dollars a week and might make
the Man mad at him for leaving his fields."

But it isn't her nature to dwell on gloom. She picks herself
up by telling stories with happy endings. A fifty-five-year-old
migrant named Ben Callaway has, through her urgings, just
deposited $5 in a bank, the first time in his life he ever put any-

thing away. A rural shack visited a few months before had no furniture except iron beds, bare walls, one curtainless window. The people responded to suggestions about fixing it up and now there is a dresser made of vegetable crates, curtains of flour sacks, pictures drawn on foil tins from ten-cent store pies. And there is Eunice Foster, thirty-five-year-old mother of nine children whose migrant husband is disabled and can no longer work. She still picks in season but she's also enrolled in the vocational courses, studying mathematics and home nursing, doing very well in multiplication and division.

So Miss Blakely and others like her administer what small doses of salvation they can to those in the Migrant Stream. For every one they help out of it, a thousand sweep by. But they have to believe that a pie tin on a shack wall is a means toward an end, that a mother learning the multiplication table of nine carries significance beyond the minor fact of scholastic achievement. What the government providing the program believes is something else and not so encouraging as Miss Blakely's dedication. Depending on her to make up in zeal what she lacked in resources, the government seems to be dropping hints of salvation in places like the Pompano Community Action office, then making it clear in a hundred ways that the hint is not to be taken seriously.

21

Journey's End

"IT is far easier, I know," W. J. Cash wrote, "to criticize the failure of the South to face and solve its problems than it is to solve them."

Southern lives in trouble bear witness to this truth: Buck Sims evicted off his land in Alabama; Mrs. Brown in Georgia patting her daughter's burn scars that will never go away; Kentuckian John B. Cooney telling how it is to be a worked-out miner unable to keep his children in school; Walter Greene patching an aged shrimp boat in South Carolina and Virgil Orange wondering if the government will loan him money so he can buy a boat of his own to patch; Mae-Troy Blakely wading back into the Florida Migrant Stream to see what she can salvage.

But beyond Cash's truth that criticism is easy and solution difficult lies another: a South and a nation that so far have failed the poor possess the capacity to succeed in bringing hope to troubled lives. With this capacity goes an imperative transcending regionalism, exerting itself on the entire country. While I made this Southern journey in the summer of 1967, Northern fires of riot and rebellion were burning in Newark and Detroit. Much of the combustible material then and in this summer of 1968 came from the rural South—poor, black, and bitter. The migration, experts say, will run at least another decade, masses moving from rural to urban poverty through corridors of plenty. It is like piping oil into a flaming well. Except that people are being consumed.

Their tragedy threatens the social order. Self-preservation, if not compassion, reasons that it is in the interest of a country whose Gross National Product now exceeds $800 billion to divert a significant share of its fortune to meet the crisis of poverty, north and south. But, as sociologist Gunnar Myrdal observes:

> Congress is much more willing to spend money on wars and war preparations than on needed improvements at home ... the even more serious fact is, however, that Congress apparently reflects how the American electorate feel toward this question of national priorities. The fact that a majority of Americans are fairly well off and do not feel the pinch of misery of the slum dwellers—except as a strange and unpleasant element in the surroundings to which they just want to close their minds— makes understandable this popular disinterest....

An already inadequate Poverty Program remained more or less intact financially as 1967 ended, but only after frantic last-minute efforts by its supporters before Congress. And even this victory was hallowed by new regulations removing the vestige of control previously permitted the poor in OEO programs and giving it over to public officials. It is inevitable that political considerations inextricably linked with racism now will further erode Poverty Program benefits to Southern Negroes. While this is a reactionary development, my experiences suggest that the Poverty Program as originally conceived could function at 100 percent efficiency and still not begin to do the job that needs to be done.

That job is tough, complex, revolutionary. The Poverty Program's passing effort at training and education, loan assistance, and community organizing is only a minor part of the job. While the work to be done is awesome, resources to see it through are ample, even abundant. The President's National Advisory Commission on Rural Poverty, after noting that "most of the rural South is one vast poverty area," affirms that "the United States has the resources and the technical means to assure every person in the United States adequate food, shelter, clothing, medical care and education and, accordingly, recommends action toward this end." But "action toward this end" involves commitments of the American will that no Congress can appropriate or agency implement. Here arise the unanswered questions that will determine success or failure—how to inspire national and regional motivation to make resources available, how to deal with the apparent fact that a majority of Americans feel that a surfeit of material things for most is compatible with deprivation for many, how to separate myths about poverty from the truth about private and governmental forces fostering it?

Faced with the magnitude of the work to be done and those hanging questions, any one person or single report claiming *the* solution to the problems of the Southern poor is at best presumptuous, at worst irresponsible. These closing pages would try to avoid those designations. But George Dawkins learning about the monkeyhood of Jo-Jo, eighty-five-year-old Donald Chestnut still plowing for $5 a day, young Joseph Wilcox bearing his physical and emotional wounds along a Tuscaloosa sidewalk—these lives require some conclusions from an observer beyond sympathy. The conclusions that follow are one man's appraisal of how conditions might be improved. Anyone with additional, better ideas is encouraged to present them, for, God knows, they are needed.

By journey's end, it seemed clear that the South's peculiar regional problems interact so intimately with the national problems that to consider them separately is to draw lines as artificial and self-defeating as those separating Georgia counties. Clear, too, that the federal government is the only American institution that can initiate reforms of sufficient scope with requisite speed. In Washington, the best and the worst of our national essence is distilled, creating concepts of progressivism which, along with funds, are lacking in Southern state governments. Because Washington has so far done badly what local governments or the private sector will not do at all, it is becoming fashionable to suggest that antipoverty efforts should be left to the states and private enterprise, with Washington merely providing tax dollars but not regulating their disbursement. Since nobody loves a federal bureaucracy, this is appealing in theory. But in practice, it does not work. Examples have been cited of states and counties providing shamefully low welfare payments under cruelly restrictive regulations despite the fact that most of the money is federal; agriculture programs are perverted to local prejudice, antipoverty programs blunted, the list is endless. At the same time, industry builds in the midst of plenty while backlands starve for commerce, or it locates in those backlands where authority assures it captive labor at negligible cost in paychecks and taxes. The theory of limiting the federal role might be persuasive were state governments responsible to all citizens, if industry were capable of selflessness. But the record reminds us of realities and the theory founders on them.

So, to begin with, the South needs an extraordinary, unified federal effort—job training and public works on the style of WPA but vaster, coordinated with health, education, welfare, and agricultural and industrialization programs. It is a simple matter to sit back and write such a sweeping prescription, and just as simple to dismiss it as an indulgence in visions of super-statism as the panacea for all ills. But present efforts and the systems behind them are unable to meet the crisis of poverty, as they have always been unable to meet it. With "good times" (and if we are not in good times now we never shall be) or "bad times," the hard core of poverty has remained, waxing or waning by a few millions, sometimes glimpsed by the national eye but more often unnoticed in its grief. America's historic ideas about how to deal with poverty are bankrupt. At the same time, a combination of national circumstances, with the Negro revolution the most important, provides an imperative to be radical in our impatience with failure. No one questions our capacity in a country that has accomplished prodigies as a matter of course; it is a matter of desire, of commitment, of a passionate vision of what America should be.

A Kentucky judge who heads the OEO effort in impoverished Leslie County put this vision into words scaled to the needs of his small section of the American landscape. Judge George Wooton is alternately politician and humanist as he tells of driving a bulldozer on Work Training Happy Pappy projects and shows off a gavel of polished mountain hemlock given to him by grateful participants.

"I know what these people here are up against," he says. "As a boy I went barefoot to school and at lunchtime we ate our bread in a tree in the schoolyard because there was a family of big hogs rooted there and they'd take the food right off you. This area has gone down, down, down. Nature floods us in the hollows and men take the resources. Our wealth is in coal and timber but outside ownership takes all the profits. But it doesn't have to be that way. Taxes could give us our share of the resources. With federal money and imagination, we could build hundreds of dams around these streams that flood us and create a series of waterway lakes for trade and tourism. The county could be planned and zoned for area-wide development instead of doing it in bits and pieces. We should move our towns and homes out of the hollows and live on the tops of these mountains, where the sun shines, where the air is cleaner and the birds sing sweeter."

There is material for such lyricism in a National Rehabilitation Program that would train men and then send them out to reclaim communities and lands too long neglected. There is work to be done in the South alone that would keep men busy for as far into the future as anyone can see—hundreds of thousands of ramshackle dwellings to be leveled and houses with stout walls and roofs and decent bathrooms built in their place; rural roads stretching in their aggregate to the moon or beyond to be paved; millions of acres nourished back into productivity; streams and rivers cleansed of pollution, dammed for flood control and power, stocked for food and sport, channeled for irrigation; schools and medical centers erected, a network of sports facilities created for all ages, and special provisions made for the growing numbers of elderly persons cut loose from their families by the customs of our age. All this is no Utopian imagining; it is a practical beginning toward making the American Dream more than an empty phrase.

This beginning requires planning and budget commitments spanning decades, and not dependent on the annual whim of Congress. It requires a total approach instead of the growing tendency toward fragmentation that produces inchoate programs, Judge Wooton's "bits and pieces." [106] An OEO school for carpenters in an area where no buildings are going up is temporary dole in the trappings of "work experience and training." But in conjunction with government plans to replace five hundred shacks in the county, it places the carpenter trainee in a meaningful partnership with society, a relationship that may endure to the benefit of both.

Inevitably, a training and public works program both massive and intricate would not be carried out always with wisdom and boldness. It is the nature of bureaucratic reform (or the preferable word, rehabilitation) to make mistakes along with progress. But, given the random nature of our various state governments, only the federal mind—discerning and responsive in comparison—is capable of the rational, compassionate planning that would give long-range direction to antipoverty efforts. The beautiful example of George Dawkins could be repeated ten thousandfold and enhanced. The ludicrous spectacle of work-hungry mountain men in Kentucky watching hillbilly movies during job training or women in Baker County Georgia, learning to sew without a factory to receive them could be eliminated. But only if the kind of scrupulous care and dedication lavished on a moon-shot is applied. For instance, to leave the location of industries purely to chance is to insure that hundreds of Southern counties will never emerge from economic limbo. Yet there is no law prohibiting the government from persuading industries to settle here or there. Industries spend millions of tax-deductible consumer dollars each year lobbying in Washington to influence the destination of government contracts. Then let the government stipulate in bids for the thousands of cars it buys each year that an assembly plant must be established in the area of X, Y, and Z counties, providing immediate jobs and all the economic rejuvenation deriving from an assured supply of weekly paychecks. A plant headed for southern California to make space suits might head instead for southern Georgia if given federal tax write-offs for specified periods. These federal write-offs would not disturb the local taxes so important to the economy of a poor county or state. But they could boom a depressed region into solvency.[107]

The governmental "persuasions" may carry unpleasant undertones of authoritarian federal controls on industry. But when one becomes intimate with the desperate need for work in Southern rural areas, those undertones are not so harsh as the overtones of industrial license that permit corporations to use America and her population as their private preserve. The American sensibility is not offended at workers being the captives of industry, often well-paid and generally satisfied, but captives nonetheless. But it balks at a portion of this industry being manipulated by the government for the common good. An alternative even more heretical would be government-built and operated factories to assure jobs for those graduating from OEO programs and others unemployed. Again, men without work seem to be a more acceptable national condition than government factories, which raise specters of socialism, communism, or, worst of all, competition. This is not the place to argue philosophies but to indicate the logic of need. These badly needed government factories might, by law, be limited to producing material to be used *only* in the nation's Rehabilitation Program—cinder block to rebuild shacks, pipe for sewer lines, floorboards for schools. It seems a modest heresy.

Innovations must be accompanied by the effective functioning of existing institutions. Does it sound reasonable that the federal government demands that rigid standards be met when it gives a state highway construction funds yet permits millions of welfare dollars to be apportioned without controls to wildly variant and generally inadequate Southern state welfare systems? A dependent child in Mississippi is given $15 a month for food and Washington shrugs. But let a highway into Jackson funded with the same percentage of federal monies as welfare exceed safety grade maximums by a surveyor's mite and Washington will quickly demand that Mississippi come up to standard.

The U.S. Public Health Service ministers to those suffering from venereal disease, leprosy, or drug addiction. But poor and sick Southerners not fortunate enough to suffer these afflictions must get well or die as best they can. While USPHS echoes its defensive shibboleth of preventative, not curative, medicine, Negro babies are dying at twice the rate of white babies in some Black Belt states and adults of both races often receive nineteenth-century medical services. There are some counties without doctors, and many counties where doctors never get into rural areas; and in almost every area the poor cannot afford their ailments. In these pages we have met persons earning $20 a week and owing more than $1,000 for operations. A bill like that means bondage for years, contracted in the name of life-saving surgical skill. For unknown and unnumbered others who lack the $50 universal down payment to enter a hospital, death comes when it might be staved off. Legions of elderly persons have never been informed about Medicare, and other legions cannot afford the $3-a-month payments. It is a barbarous situation in a country undeniably rich and purportedly civilized.

The USPHS should institute a major recruitment and scholarship program to train thousands of doctors and nurses who would agree to serve for specified periods in areas where they are needed. This is a nation woefully short of doctors for all the American Medical Association's claim of providing the best doctoring in the world.[108] Again, a system has failed and there is nothing revolutionary in proposing another approach. The Armed Services keep supplied with doctors through just such education-exchanged-for-service programs. Is there something inherently evil in the government's caring for sick civilians along with its soldiers? Or does the AMA have the right to insist that all medicine must be for profit, even if it means that the ability to pay can determine who will live and who will die, who will suffer and who will be made well?

The story of the Department of Agriculture's poverty-creating role in the South, particularly in relation to Negro farmers, has been documented by the U.S. Civil Rights Commission and others.[109] It is a sorry record of denying counsel, loans, and crop allotments to those who need them most, of abetting racial discrimination, and of insuring through programs favoring large landowners that small white and Negro farmers will have to leave the land. Secretary Freeman, who describes the rural migration northward as "lemming-like" and in the next breath talks of making rural America so rich in opportunities that by the year 2000 "many of the 100 million additional people we shall have can choose to live in the countryside if they wish. As President Johnson said, 'We must give these millions of people a right of choice where to live.'" The hypocritical contrast between the Department's words and its practices does not inspire confidence in future reform. When Secretary Freeman must stage a politically dictated "drive by" of a Negro co-op in Alabama rather than risk offending whites with a visit, then it must be acknowledged that the Department of Agriculture is so afflicted with schizophrenic tensions that it cannot move resolutely in the direction it needs to go.

That direction leads toward an unprecedented program of "land and loans" for the rural poor backed by a department marketing philosophy not geared exclusively to the profit goals of big-time agribusiness operators. The South—and other regions —needs land reform if the agrarian poverty cycle spiraling from one generation to the next is ever to be broken. Nothing less. The United States is a champion of land reform (in theory, at least) when it applies to Latin America or South Vietnam, but suffers a curious loss of agrarian vision inside its own borders. Clarity should begin at home. Perhaps the reason it doesn't is because to enunciate a program of land reform implies that vast numbers of landless peasants exist and this admission does not befit a power that spends $4.4 billion a year covering the land with highways.

Here is a country with 70 percent of its 200 million people crowded onto one percent of the land, mostly in deteriorating urban centers. The drift from farm to city is universally bewailed. Yet, let someone propose a scheme to foster small, family farms as a means of keeping people on the land and it is denounced as financially unworkable, romantically impractical, socialistic, or a precursor to communes. The arguments against subsistence farming have been heard down through the years. Now it is time to hear something else: America, if only in self-defense, must right generations of wrongs committed against the landless by providing them with the earth, tools, and logistics required to fashion decent agrarian lives. Many landless are men like Joe Chester of Baker County, Georgia. He is content to spend his life farming to care for his growing family. Then let him have a farm carved out of all those ample acres on those ducal preserves of quail and pine that cover half the county. He is not to blame because he was born poor and landless and indentured to a system that has created a race of black hired hands in the South. And not a few white ones, too.

With one hundred or so acres provided Chester from the

Ischaway Plantation's twenty-five thousand, where he now works, he would have a start on a farm that could provide for his family and turn a small profit. It might even enable his children to escape the flight to the cities that he sees as their only future, or at least send them off better prepared in mind and body. The cost to the federal government would not be prohibitive when ranged beside the fiscal and spiritual costs the country is paying each time a Joe Chester is forced off the land. Given the assessed valuation of the plantation, acquisition costs would be tolerably, even ridiculously, low. Loans would have to be made to get Chester going, but subsistence purchase prices are modest for needs like seed and fertilizer. A shoat costs a few dollars and within a year becomes a four-hundred-pound hog that dresses down to three hundred pounds of pork for a family. Chicks cost a few cents each and in ten weeks they are broilers ready to market or eat. A few hundred dollars buys a milk cow to provide the fresh milk that Chester's children need and do not get. If the government doesn't want him in the cotton complex and can't afford to provide him with the tractor that would let him diversify into soybean farming or some other specialty, then a communal tractor could be provided for a group of families, as Joe Johnson's co-op hopes to do. Communal pastures might enable poor farmers to make their long-denied move into livestock operations.

If states can use their right of eminent domain to acquire land for highways built with federal funds, there is no legal reason why the Ischaway Plantation should be off limits to agrarian progress. The principle of the government opening land to those who need it seems a thoroughly American one recalling the days of homesteading; or the Freedman's Bureau after the Civil War.[110] Land title is not a right divinely conferred; it is a very human device, and if title searches were not confined to the realms of legal documents but extended into moral regions where time obscures histories of fraud, exploitation, chicanery, and greed, then deeds could tell stories about the land far more interesting than dry covenants describing "all that certain plot, piece or parcel of land, with the buildings and improvements thereon erected, situate, lying and being in the...." But if true tales of land acquisition must be relegated to history as a practical necessity, the present imperative to redistribute land should not be prejudiced by the notion that property is sacrosanct. Only the right of people to live decently should be inviolable.

So, appropriate large holdings can be legally acquired through purchase and parceled out to those poor who want to remain on the land. The poorest would require outright gifts of land and the seed, fertilizer, and stock needed to begin balanced farming. With others, long-term, low-interest loans could replace grants. Combinations of both approaches would have to be tried along with cooperative experimentation to determine how best to utilize a national system of small farms. Some families would certainly require yearly subsidies to augment subsistence farming. Big, corporate growers, particularly in the West, are receiving millions in hidden subsidies each year through irrigation water supplied by state and federal governments. Why this corporate aid should be any more in the national interest than payments to individual farmers is a question going to the heart of our national purpose, and how it is answered in Washington during the coming years will determine whether any real change is ever to be made on the landscape of the rural poor. No one sorting over the evidence of the results of mass migration to the cities over recent decades, no one counting the emotional costs to these displaced Americans and material costs to society in welfare, nonproductivity, and disorder should dismiss the idea of direct rural subsidies. If a guaranteed annual wage or something similar proves an urban need, then the principle established for the city is equally valid for the farm. No amount of federal planning and execution can completely reverse the twentieth-century movement from the farm to cities. The magnetism of the town is an age-old pull on man in any century and particularly in this one with its stress on ease and leisure, which are not characteristic of farm life. But human values can shift, and the physical and moral blight of American cities may induce coming generations to reappraise the geography of the good life. However, if Joe Chester's sons are to be kept down on the farm, farming must promise them more than the pittance it gave to their father. For their sake and for the sake of a hungry world waiting to be fed, the Department of Agriculture and the Congress have to end their rhetoric of concern over small farmers and the rural poor and move with a spirit of compassion and a sense of urgency to end their neglect and restore purpose to lives too long without it.

These closing pages are studded with the words "should," "must," "requires," "could," "are needed," and so on. At a time when blacks and whites in the South and the rest of the country seem to be moving irresistibly toward racial Armageddon, when many blacks have lost faith in reform and many whites revert to historic arrogance and disdain for the poor of whatever color, these words seem pretentious if not futile. While the individual stories of Southern poor in this survey suggest that certain remedies may be logical, logic has never been man's primary preoccupation in America or anywhere else. Our will to act is more dependent on emotion, prejudice, and a "felt" sense of what is right than it is on dispassionate—or even passionate— analysis. While this is a universal human condition, the results in America seem less justifiable, even intolerable when ranged beside our resources and philosophies, and the hope they once inspired in common men everywhere. It may be that, despite those noble philosophies and our statistics of abundance, the ultimate American history will be a record of resources plundered and hopes betrayed by the arrogance of affluence. Perhaps we expected too much from our beginnings, revered heroic words while overlooking actions that belied them, made a pioneer virtue of rapaciousness that took land from Indians, farmed it with slaves, and mortgaged it to the concept of profit at any price. That concept was incompatible with the Christianity we professed, but the dilemma was resolved by not scrutinizing too closely the moral ingredients of financial success and not questioning whether success for some was related to misery for others. Mixing with these traditions of behavior were impulsive generosity, great energy, and stunning initiative. The result is our heritage of wealth and poverty, power and weakness, and all the myths surrounding them.

Probably the most powerful myth is that of the self-made man, powerful because once there was much truth in it and there always will be some. But upward mobility for the poor-but-honest boy seeking opportunity isn't what it used to be in American society (and never was for Negroes).

Today, the relation of a man to his institutions of education and commerce is largely defined from birth, individual exceptions still being possible but the mass of lives following patterns they are born to. Still, the myth dies hard because it is flattering for anyone who has gotten somewhere to believe it was all his doing. The corollary is that if someone hasn't made it, it's all *his* doing too. So the status quo, however inhumane, is justified and the justification reinforced by the awful authority of the familiar: That's the way things have always been and you can't change human nature. Men who benefit from the status quo cite this authority as a talisman against change, predicting terrible consequences in its wake, raising the popular wrath against innovators and often convincing those most needful that change is evil. These forces of "felt" logic and the tyranny of custom are particularly strong in the South, working against a radical attack on poverty. Their influence, at a time when most Southern whites are making do better than ever before, requires that the question be asked: Do you white people who own most of the land and control most of the region's wealth and wealth-producing mechanisms feel an obligation to alter the status quo if it would eradicate poverty, whose most bereft victims are black?

The answer seems to be "No." Sanctimonious declarations of good intention, the interposition of modification, and disclaimers of responsibility may be offered by officials, editors, and men in the street. But rhetoric, however gorgeous or mean, winnows down to "No." Racism has blunted white sensibility to black poverty while the fact that the white poor have always been with us is converted into the dictum that they always should be. At a time when the sons of the poor of both races are doing most of the fighting and dying in Vietnam, this response is (and the abused word for once assumes validity) un-American. It mocks both the concept of brotherhood and nationhood. In a just and true nation, men feel themselves brothers and each suffers hurt to another. This is only an ideal but the ideals we pursue determine what we are and what we shall become. Our present ideals are murky; our future clouded.

We rocket toward the moon and leave the earth in grief. We speed in supercars through the Southern landscape past the ubiquitous shack that blurs in our eye and conscience. Someone is in that shack. If we deny him, we deny ourselves and make our nationhood a fiction. The man in that shack is no anonymous beggar holding out a battered hat for a dole, no stranger from an alien land trying to establish squatter's rights in the heart of our concern. Whether he speaks in the dry mountain accent of eastern Kentucky or a liquid Black Belt drawl, we know him. He is a son of America and our brother.

Yours and mine.

Notes

[1] *Hungry Children,* Southern Regional Council special report on doctors' investigation of the Mississippi Delta: "In sum, we saw children who are hungry and who are sick—children for whom hunger is a daily fact of life and sickness, in many forms, an inevitability.... They are suffering from hunger and disease and directly or indirectly they are dying from them—which is exactly what 'starvation' means."

[2] But, predictably, not in Mississippi. The Jackson *Daily News* featured a letter from a woman reader saying in part: "I am indignant. Mississippians are indignant.... This report, founded on misinformation and misstatement, was distorted, exaggerated beyond comprehension.... Since time immemorial, planters have taken care of the medical needs of their tenants.... One doctor said he visited a Negro home where the six children had beans for dinner, biscuits and molasses for supper—and nothing else! I do not doubt this in the least—it is what they like."

[3] And not just the province of the South. Agriculture Secretary Orville Freeman in a letter of April 26, 1967, to Senator Joseph Clark noted that while Mississippi led the nation in the number of poor people getting federal food, close behind in second place was—New York!

[4] Citizens Crusade vs. Poverty report of June, 1967, carried government figures showing that in fifteen Southern and border states, 3 million classified as poor lived in 93 counties with no food programs, while in 190 counties with programs, food was going to only 1,029,331 of 7,100,367 poor. Overall, 1 million of 10 million were getting food. In the year since then, there has been considerable improvement in some states. But the overwhelming majority of Southern poor still do not receive federal food.

[5] Beale, *The Negro in American Agriculture,* p. 189: "in 1960 more than half (57) percent of all Southern nonwhite farm boys aged 14 and 15 were retarded in school. That is to say, they had not reached the grades

that are normal for persons their age. The corresponding proportion for white farm boys that age was 26 percent in the South and only 11 percent in the North and West. Even more astonishing is the fact that of the nonwhite farm boys who were behind in school a substantial majority had fallen two or more years behind. In most instances, retardation becomes a prelude to quitting school altogether . . . and 3/4 of all Negro farm boys do drop out before completing high school."

[6] In eastern Kentucky, for example, where poverty is virtually all-white, nearly a quarter of the inhabitants over twenty-four cannot read and write.

[7] The states forfeiting federal aid to children, blind, aged, and disabled are Alabama, Mississippi, Arkansas, Florida, Georgia, Kentucky, Texas, Maryland, Missouri, Louisiana, North Carolina, South Carolina, and Tennessee. While forfeiting millions, most of these states pay unbelievably low monthly benefits to those poor people who manage to qualify despite rigorous and often illegal efforts by state welfare officials to keep them off the rolls. Alabama, for example, forfeits $28 million while paying an average monthly benefit of *$12.97 per needy person.* Georgia passes up $31 million, pays an average benefit of $12.11; Arkansas $12 million against a *$4.17* payment. Interestingly, Maryland, which forfeited only $1 million, pays out a respectable $69.15 average to welfare clients.

[8] "Traditionally, benefits have been denied to families if the husband is present and 'employable' (whether or not he can get a job). Unemployed husbands therefore 'desert,' and mothers may then get on relief (if they agree to sue for nonsupport). But often the men remain near the families, despite the danger of being apprehended and jailed for nonsupport. Welfare departments maintain squads of investigators who track down these men, sometimes by invading homes between midnight and dawn without warrants. . . . An especially vicious feature of these rules is that if a caseworker judges that such a man 'appears' to exist, the burden of proving that he is not a 'substitute' father falls on the mother." Cloward and Piven, *New Republic* (August 5, 1967).

[9] See prepared statement of Dr. Britton, Committee print of the Subcommittee on Employment, Manpower and Poverty of the Committee on Labor and Public Welfare, July 1, 1967.

[10] Vivian Henderson, *The Economic Status of Negroes in the Nation and in the South* in Southern Regional Council's series "Toward Regional Realism—No. 3, 1963."

[11] There is a 700-page thick catalogue, dwarfing those of Sears and Montgomery Ward combined, subtitled "A description of the Federal government's domestic programs to assist the American people in furthering their social and economic progress."

[12] An Associated Press story of March 18, 1967, says the federal govern-

ment spends an estimated $425 million a year on publicity. "[This] is more than double the combined outlay for news gathering by the two major U.S. news services, the three major television networks and the 10 biggest American newspapers," observes the AP. The military spends the most—at least $32.3 million—with the National Aeronautics and Space Agency accounting for $11.5 million. The Department of Agriculture is a big spender on publicity, nearly $9 million, and even hard-up OEO takes $2.4 million from its antipoverty funds and diverts it to flackery. The total AP estimate of $425 million for governmental publicity is more than the South received in poverty funds during 1967.

[13] Former Defense Secretary McNamara, speaking in 1967, in Montreal, pointed out that since 1958, only one of twenty-seven rich nations had a major internal upheaval while thirty-two of thirty-eight very poor nations averaged two violent outbreaks each year. It was not clear whether the United States was the one rich nation he referred to, but Secretary McNamara concluded: "There is an irrefutable relationship between violence and economic backwardness. And the trend of such violence is up, not down. When people are hungry and poor, they look toward any promise of a better life."

[14] In Glascock County, Georgia, officials refused to accept a food stamp program although the county has widespread poverty. Sheriff John L. English said: "There'd be just a lot of niggers lined up there and that's all it'd do. If there's anybody in the state of Georgia that goes to bed hungry it's just because he's sorry as hell."

[15] Sumter is the thirty-sixth poorest county in the United States with an annual per capita income of $585, yet officials would not allow any federal food program—either free commodities or stamps—to operate. Many Negroes there take this as proof that the whites do not so much want them to die of hunger as they want to starve them out of the county to assure perpetuation of white political supremacy. Statistical source: U.S. Census Bureau.

[16] Beale, *op. cit.* The Department of Agriculture also reports total U.S. tenant farms down from 2,364,923 in 1940 to 537,899 in 1964.

[17] Speech by Agriculture Secretary Freeman quoting President Johnson: "Not just sentiment demands that we do more to help our farms and rural communities... the welfare of this Nation demands it.... Must we export our youth to the cities faster than we export our crops and livestock? I believe we can do something about this."

[18] Beale, *op. cit.*, p. 187: "In each major tenure class—full owners, part owners and tenants—the average age of nonwhite Southern farmers is older than that of white farmers.... The farms operated by Negroes have historically been small. With their limited capital, Negroes were lucky to

acquire land at all, let alone buy a large place.... In 1935 ... the average size of a Negro-operated farm was 44 acres; white farmers averaged 131. As the ability and necessity to have larger units grew, the size of white farms grew ... by 1959, the white average had nearly doubled, rising to 249 acres. Among Negro farmers little of this trend is evident. Although hundreds of thousands of small tenant units have disappeared, the average size ... has gone up to only 52 acres, an increase of just 8 acres since 1935."

[19] U.S. Commission on Civil Rights report, *Equal Opportunity in Farm Programs,* 1965: "The Commission's analysis of four major USDA programs (ASCS, Farmers Home Administration, Federal Extension Service and Soil Conservation Service) has clearly indicated that the Department has generally failed to assume responsibility for assuring equal opportunity and equal treatment to all those entitled to benefit from its programs."

[20] "... in many areas county government operations are dwarfed by ASCS programs as measured in dollar expenditures or impact on residents or both." Professor Morton Grodzins in *Review of Farmers Committee Systems.*

[21] The New York *Times,* August 11, 1967: "Armin Rosenkranz, a Washington lawyer who helped win the [ASCS] election delay, illustrated the Alabama problem by citing what he called an actual case. A white man and a Negro were farming the same crop, cotton, side by side. The Negro had 100 acres, the white man 50. The county committee took 80 of the Negro's acres out of production but let the white farmer produce on all 50...."

[22] Figures from the National Sharecroppers League.

[23] *Southern Courier,* May 20, 1967.

[24] His experience helps to explain why the number of Negro tenant farmers in Sumter County dropped from 2,240 in 1945 to 702 in 1964. The nationwide exodus of black and white from farms was also occurring, with Sumter part of the phenomenon. Yet, oppressive conditions peculiar to blacks speak for themselves as a specific reason for flight.

[25] Alabama welfare law and its implementation seems designed to thwart rather than aid the indigent. Of total federal funds forfeited, Alabama lost $11.6 million earmarked for needy children in 1966, $12.2 million in 1967.

[26] This may or may not have been true. The Southwest has been receiving the lion's share of allotments in recent years. Its big-business, computerized, mechanized, and sure-fire profit-making approach to cotton appeals strongly to the merchandising instincts of the Department of Agriculture. Arizona, California, New Mexico, and western Texas with their flat lands and dry climate designed for irrigation and machine-farming

produced only 2 percent of the cotton in 1919; it is 34 percent now and rising. But while taking from the less efficient (bearing their burden of history) and giving to the capitalized, efficient few might be good business, it might not be good government. This radical notion has not been allowed to disturb the myopic vision of the Department of Agriculture.

The squeeze in Greene County on Lewis Hood is roughly the same as exists in Sumter County next door and for which statistics are available. They show that after a major reapportionment of cotton allotments in 1964, the average total Negro allotment was 11.9 acres, the average white 61.4. Even allowing for the disparity in black-white acreage, black still trailed proportionally in allotments. It should be understood that an acre of cotton grosses at most $150. Hood, cut to 3 acres, might realize $450 for his year's work *before expenses.*

27 Birmingham *News,* June 30, 1967: "They [the Negroes] nodded in agreement as he explained his department's policy of non-discrimination in its program.... They obviously appreciated Freeman's personal attention and the fact that he left a top aide behind to take down complaints and suggestions." Freeman was in the church fifteen minutes.

28 Freeman would seem in conflict with his own directive of June 23, 1964: "Government public information programs, educational activities and services of a like character should be available to all persons on an equal basis. Care must be exercised that acceptance of speaking engagements and participation in conferences by Federal officials is consistent with this policy. Officials should not participate in conferences or speak before audiences where any racial group has been segregated or excluded...."

29 It would have been an appropriate question, to judge from the Civil Rights Commission report cited previously. It found Negro children barred from 4-H activities offered to whites with, for example, only 3 percent of black youngsters receiving citizenship training which 90 percent of whites received. In counties without Negro agents there were no programs at all. Negro agents consistently were given less training in courses where they were segregated from their white counterparts. "... in Alabama in January, 1964 white agents received 2 days of cotton training well before the beginning of the cotton planting season. Negro agents covered the same subject in half a day in April." The report continued: "Segregation has permeated extension activities in three crucial areas—planning, personnel and services. Furthermore it has occurred at all three levels of government—Federal, State and county... the Federal Extension Service, by acquiescing in the determination by others of what Negroes should and should not receive in many counties of the South, has often permitted Negro farmers and rural residents to be partially deprived or wholly cut

off from those benefits which the agency was originally established to provide."

While USDA directives since then have ordered this situation improved, the degree of implementation varies and the effect in the field is not generally apparent. The handicap to Negro farmers discriminated against over the years by these programs is all too apparent in outmoded farming techniques, decreased productivity, and low standard of living.

[30] Henderson, *op. cit.*: "Whereas just a few years ago the large majority of [Southern] Negroes lived on farms, today about 72 percent live in urban areas and about one-half live in the central cities of those urban areas." Every Southern state except Florida has experienced a decline in Negro rural population and every Southern state including Florida has experienced a tremendous increase in Negro urban population. Henderson shows that between 1950 and 1960, for example, Negro urban populations increased by 31.4 percent in Georgia, 23.1 in Alabama, 71.3 in Florida, and 210.7 in Louisiana. As he subsequently demonstrates, job opportunities for blacks were shrinking instead of stretching as they came off the farm.

[31] *Ibid.*: "In every category except 'government,' Negroes had a smaller share of the jobs in 1960 than in 1950 in the South." Henderson's tables go on to show that black employment in manufacturing dropped 21.3, in transportation 13.7, in construction 4.5. But for women like Mrs. Wilcox and her mother, opportunities were maintained. The percentage of nonwhite women in household work—44.7—was exactly the same in 1960 as 1950, while the percentage in service work like restaurants rose 3.1 to 20.8. Nonwhite males in service and unskilled labor also rose a few points to 36.3 of the total force. But in white-collar occupations, the decade saw an increase only of from 5.8 to 8.3. Decimals neatly measure deprivation.

[32] Whites at Bryce Mental Hospital, which ex-Governor Wallace refuses to desegregate in successful defiance of federal law, are only a little better off. *Southern Courier* reporter Robin Reisig on July 8, 1967, noted that there were only twenty-two doctors (five psychiatrists) for 5,000 patients. On August 14, 1967, the New York *Times,* reporting criticism of Matteawan State Mental Hospital in Beacon, New York, provided a contrast in standards with its headline: FIND ONLY 14 PSYCHIATRISTS SERVING 600 PATIENTS.

[33] An individual ultimately is responsible for his personal life. But influences can't be discounted. The federal government tries to influence rural families for the good through the Federal Extension Service, which, we have noted, is unequally administered by the states. It is not to remove all responsibility from Mrs. Wilcox, product of an Alabama tenant farm, for her apparent inability to cope. But responsibility must be shared. The U.S. Civil Rights Commission pointed out, for example, that Alabama

State Extension Service home demonstration programs in 1960 found instruction in family living reaching 24 percent of white rural households, 10 percent Negro; clothing, 44 and 19 percent; home management, 20 and 9 percent; food and nutrition, 47 and 22 percent.

34 Address: Route 1, Box 72, Alberta, Alabama 36720.

35 Despite the relative prosperity of Selma today in comparison to other small Southern cities and despite civil rights activism to an unparalleled degree, poverty remains endemic to more than 60 percent of the Negro population. Dallas County officials, however, refused federal food until Washington threatened to give it to civil rights leaders to distribute.

36 *Narrative Summary of the Economic Opportunity Amendments of 1966:* "Furthermore, no program shall be approved or continued after March 1 [1967] which is not conducted, administered, or coordinated by a board on which representatives of the poor make up at least one third of the membership."

37 W. L. Cash, *The Mind of the South* (New York, Knopf, 1941), p. 435: "The result is that the body of the South has inevitably been confirmed in complacency and illusion. In large part, efforts to call attention to the problems which exist have been treated not only as an unnecessary attempt at trouble-making but as a gross affront to the section."

38 OEO offices invariably are in small, temporary quarters, a reminder if any were needed of the program's impermanent and under-funded status in the government.

39 On January 18, 1965, Dr. King was attacked in the lobby by a member of the National States Rights Party while breaking the hotel's century-old color line. In the weeks that followed, 2,500 civil rights demonstrators were arrested in Selma.

40 U.S. Civil Rights Commission, *op. cit.*: "Although Negroes in 1959 comprised 16 percent of the farm operators in the South, they operated less than 4 percent of the farmland. Even white cropper-operated farms (economically the lowest tenure class) averaged 68 acres while farms operated by Negro full owners had an average of only 62 acres. The economic distance separating Negro and white farm families is clearly illustrated by the fact that in 1959 the *highest average level of living index for Negro farmers* in any of the 14 states studied *was lower than the lowest state average* level of living index *of white farmers*."

41 *Ibid.*: "The assistance rendered to Negroes by FHA in the form of loans and technical assistance is consistently different from that furnished to whites in the same economic class: Negro borrowers receive smaller loans, both absolutely and in relation to their net worth, than white farmers similarly situated. While carefully supervised white borrowers receive most of their funds for capital investments, including farm improve-

ment or enlargement, Negroes in the same economic class, with drastically unequal supervision, receive loans primarily for living expenses and annual operating costs."

The significance of this finding should be impressed on those who think poverty is simple. It means, among other things, that white farmers got money-producing loans for tractors and land, Negroes to pay debts and keep alive another year.

[42] The Wallaces and other Alabama Democrats favored white roosters. This was the party symbol appearing on ballots with the legend: White Supremacy for the Right. Until 1966 the state's few Negro voters casting Democratic ballots had to endure this racial affront. As black registration increased after passage of the Voting Rights Act, vote-conscious white politicians dropped the legend. But the rooster remained.

[43] Although the co-op was running in January, 1967, with the impressive total of 700 farmers, the federally subsidized Agricultural Extension Service did not contact or service it in any way until July 11, well past the planting season. At that time, Agent C. D. Scott II sent *forty* copies of a letter describing control of cucumber beetles and nematodes. The timing of this communication assumes significance a few pages hence.

[44] The Reverend Walter could not resist writing this paragraph in his Inter-religious Project newsletter: "One could discern here and there the working of Sargent Shriver's mind. All charges by the Black Belt politicians were examined minutely. If the mayor of Selma had charged that little green men operating from space ships moored in Bogue Chitto were controlling Negroes by laser beams, Shriver would have waited another week for the Air Force to check it out."

[45] Agriculture Secretary Freeman missed a chance to see the office and grading operation during his June 28 visit to Alabama. In the process, a new form of bureaucratic fecklessness called the "drive-by" was devised. Osborne had invited Freeman to see how the co-op was making out. The Birmingham *News* on July 2 provided a perceptive account of what it called Freeman's "drive-by" of the Interlaken Gin and SWAFCA:

"Freeman had been repeatedly urged by white elected officials to either ignore the co-op ... or go there to investigate charges of incompetent management and possible subversive influences in its leadership. Freeman solved this knotty political problem by inviting a spokesman for SWAFCA [Osborne] to board the secretary's chartered bus outside of Selma and give the Freeman party a briefing on the co-op's plans and operations. Then, instead of stopping at the co-op plant, Freeman simply had his bus driven by the site on the way to an airplane departure at Craig Air Force Base. Thus, he allowed the SWAFCA manager, Calvin Osborne, to claim a partial 'victory.'

"At the same time, the secretary left his route plans substantially un-changed and he did not keep waiting (due to a minor concession to SWAFCA) the two prominent local officials who greeted him briefly at Craig AFB: Dallas County Probate Judge B. A. Reynolds and Selma Mayor Joe Smitherman. It is plain Freeman did not get elected governor of Minnesota three times without absorbing some political savvy."

Thus, the Secretary of Agriculture of the United States of America, who said he wanted to find out "what must be done to enable private citizens and local officials to build modern, self-sufficient communities of tomorrow in the countryside," did not visit the first co-op of migration-prone poor Negro farmers in the history of Alabama. But Freeman's "drive-by" may have had some effect. Three weeks later those Extension Service letters [see note 43] on cucumber beetles were mailed.

46 Beale, *op. cit.*, p. 186: "Another facility of importance to a farmer is the paved or improved road. It improves his marketing ability and re-duces his degree of isolation. . . . In the South as a whole, 43 percent of all commercial scale (farms selling a minimum of $2500 a year) nonwhite farmers were still located on a dirt or unimproved road in 1959, compared with 28 percent for commercial white farmers. The disparity was even greater for the noncommercial group. . . . Negro districts in the South have seldom received standard levels of public roads from the governing au-thorities. For thousands of Negro farmers a poor road is one more handi-cap they must carry . . ."

47 The National Sharecroppers League, citing various government re-ports, reveals that in 1964 *no* Negro served on any state ASCS board in the South. By February, 1967, and in the wake of Washington "directives," there was a total of five—one Negro each in Alabama, Arkansas, Georgia, South Carolina and Mississippi. As of December, 1966, there were 49,538 ASC county office employees in Southern state offices. Of these, only 216 were Negroes in permanent positions, with another 2,886 temporarily hired in summer although a quarter of all farmers served were Negroes. In other words, while at most 6 percent of Southern ASCS employees were Negroes, 25 percent of farmers were Negroes, and in March, 1965, a fed-eral directive said: "In each state the goal will be to achieve a minority group employment percentage equal to the percentage of nonwhite farmers in the state."

48 *Ibid.*: "At the end of 1964, out of 37,000 community committeemen elected to 7,400 community committees in the South, only about 75 were Negroes. At the end of 1966 there were 543 community committeemen who were Negroes—113 in regular positions and *430 in alternate positions*. Of over 5000 county committeemen, *Negroes hold no regular positions* and only two alternate positions . . . in Georgia." The U.S. Civil Rights Com-

mission reported after April, 1968, hearings in Alabama that there still was not a single ASCS black county committeeman in the South.

[49] The New York *Times,* April 12, 1967 reported on Johnson in Washington and Alabama political opposition to the grant. Ironically, beside this account of the efforts of poor farmers to get government help was a one-inch story about the most heavily subsidized industry in the nation —oil. Depletion allowances, tax benefits, and many hidden subsidies amount to *billions* each year. The story simply said that Phillips Petroleum had doubled its assets in ten years to $2.6 billion.

[50] *Beale, op. cit.,* p. 179: "The Department of Agriculture figures as a rule of thumb that a farmer must sell at least $10,000 of products annually if he expects to make a minimum net income of $2500, and that he needs $2500 of net income to maintain a minimum decent level of living.... If $10,000 of sales is accepted as the minimum adequate scale...then only 1.3 percent of all nonwhite farms in the South were adequate size."

[51] Secretary of Agriculture Freeman, envisioning farming in the year 2000, a favorite theme in his pep talks to farmers: "Whirling overhead will be the agricultural space satellites that will supply the basic intelligence for agriculture. While the farmers of tomorrow study reports in their air-conditioned offices...relieved at last of the physical drudgery and occupational anxiety so traditionally theirs...these shiny space satellites, equipped with the most sophisticated remote sensing instruments...their sensors able to detect differences in soil...are supplying the information needed to make the key decisions."

[52] Ghettos like Watts in Los Angeles, Hough in Cleveland, and Chicago's West Side have heavy percentages of Southern migrants. It is impossible to gather figures on how many of these are jobless or underemployed, or how many took part in the riots. But by all the evidence of experience, migrants are in the most desperate economic condition and have been a significant, possibly determinant, factor in some riots.

[53] Beale, *op. cit.,* p. 178: "Throughout the South the agricultural colleges and other shapers of farming trends have long been preaching the theme of a 'green revolution'—that is, conversion of lands to hay crops and improved pastures and the raising of more livestock. This movement clearly came of age in the 1950's for the 1959 census revealed that the South as a region for the first time had more livestock farms than cotton farms. But for the Negro farmer it is almost as though such a change had never occurred. Only 4 percent of the nonwhite Southern farmers were livestock specialists...."

[54] *Ibid.,* p. 168: "...in areas of the South where he has historically been concentrated in a few traditional field crops—cotton, tobacco and peanuts

—the Negro farmer often finds himself unwelcome in other enterprises which might have been rather exclusively the white man's province. . . . For example, the only feasible way to market some specialty crops may be through cooperatives and the Negro may find that the co-op will not handle his crops. In other instances the Negro farmer may be unable to obtain credit for any but his traditional enterprises, in some cases through nothing more malicious than a lack of confidence of lenders that he can succeed. . . ."

The Civil Rights Commission cites a Federal Extension Service official saying that Negroes "have gone about as far as they can go."

55 The economic particulars at Mr. Fergurson's factory are not known to the writer. But the general attitude toward labor, especially in smaller Southern cities and towns, has not altered greatly since W. L. Cash (*op. cit.,* p. 357) wrote: "The mills were their owners' to do with wholly as they pleased, without regard to anything but their own will. . . . The master of the mill had the right to set wages and hours at whatever figure he chose. And if the workman didn't like them—this was a free country and it was his right to reject them or to quit. And if that in practise meant his right to starvation for himself and his wife and children? Let him take what he could get, save his money and he wouldn't have to put up with it for long. A lot of rich men had started poor, hadn't they?"

56 The weak state of Southern unionism has many causes that should not be oversimplified. But some are easily identifiable. A glut of cheap labor, white and Negro, as people sought escape from a faltering agrarian economy is one. Coincident with this was an urge toward industrialization which, as Cash points out (p. 437), politicians, businessmen, and even many common men felt "must be carried forward at any cost and on any terms, and that cheap labor must be maintained as the primary essential condition. All the states have redoubled their efforts to attract industries from the North or to persuade local capital to build factories by holding out extravagant and often questionable inducements."

While that was written in the late thirties, this year the Alabama State Planning and Industrial Development Board ran an ad asking, "Who's behind the $1.8 billion investment in Alabama plants in the last 4 years?" The answer was "acute executives, like you. . . . You study the reasons behind the booming, expanding economy in opportunity-loaded Alabama. . . . You find astounding financing plans let you put up plants and keep your capital funds intact. You sample community attitudes and compare Alabama's tax rates."

The ad omits mentioning one essential ingredient in this corporative happy hunting ground—an ample supply of cheap and tractable labor, either unorganized or in unions often docile due to the prevailing atmosphere historically unsympathetic to strikes and to pressures from their members fearful that militancy might lose them everything. While some states like Alabama have made notable industrial gains, the gains in too many cases have been made at the expense of laboring men like Mr. Fergurson who do not share in the paper prosperity. The overall industrialization picture in the poorest states still is spotty, more often than not dismal in the most needful regions. Alabama's advertised progress in no small measure is beneficiary of federal space age development around Huntsville. Why the federal government does not insist that similar contracts be carried out throughout the South rather than concentrated in Texas and California is a pertinent question in any discussion of Southern poverty.

[57] Most of the counties are classified 5b by the Area Redevelopment Act. This classification means that median average family income is $1,560 and median income of farm families $1,170 (both well under poverty levels) and that 60 percent or more of commercial farms are Class VI, the lowest classification, with annual sales from $50 to $2,449.

[58] The Pineland and Ischaway plantations cover 35,000 and 25,000 acres respectively. Land valuation is based on ancient assessments bearing little relation to current values and tax rates are a joke—on the noncorporate county residents.

[59] God knows what people in Burke County, Georgia, were doing. Seventy-one percent there—mostly Negroes—are classified poor and the per capita income annually is $629. This is only a few dollars higher than many Latin American countries receiving Food for Peace contributions, which Washington does not send to Burke over the objections of white people running the county, which has refused commodities. Until 1967, only 170,413 of an estimated 1,333,900 poor in Georgia received any federal food. A new state welfare director, William Beirson, has now brought food programs into all but 11 of the state's 68 counties.

[60] Beale, *op. cit.*, p. 193: "As a group they are the closest approximation that the United States has to a pariah class. . . . In the South, where Negro farmers comprise one-sixth of all farmers, Negro workers do fully one half of all farm wage work. . . . In April 1950 the South had 392,000 hired white farm workers and 298,000 nonwhites. Ten years later, the white workers had declined to 308,000 . . . nonwhites had increased to 311,000."

[61] Beale, *op. cit.*

[62] New York *Times*, September 23, 1967.

[63] The report continued: "Many [Negroes] suspect that the FHA and other lending institutions are encouraging them to dispose of rather than to develop their land holdings. This denial begins in early childhood when they are excluded from 4-H Club work and continues in later life when

they are excluded from programs of the Extension Service and from services of specialists in FHA and ASCS."

[64] And certainly not just Baker's TRAP. As sociologist Gunnar Myrdal has said: "The various policy actions rapidly improvised under the 'poverty program' were spurious, not always well administered, and, as I said, certainly not carefully planned as the inauguration of a long-term national effort to realize the demands of the national ideals." Speech, October 2, 1967, before the American Institute of Planners, Washington, D.C.

[65] Few would quarrel with this beginning. But why the rest of the gibberish, reading like a Jerry Lewis scenario, should be inflicted on persons with problems enough to begin with should be explained by the Follett Publishing Co., which prints this Basic Text, or those in the OEO program in Washington who chose it.

[66] USDA: "During 1967, USDA will finance over $300 million in loans and grants for construction improvements of some 1,700 rural water and waste disposal systems."

Where is all this good work going? Beale, *op. cit.,* says: "... by 1960 the majority of both the farm and nonfarm white rural houses [over 60 percent] had installed heated running water. On the other hand, only 2 percent of Southern farm Negro homes and 5 percent of other rural Negro homes had a modern water supply in 1950. During the 1950's, a little progress was made as the proportion with piped hot and cold water rose to 10 percent of the farm homes and 16 percent of the nonfarm rural homes ... the improvement is so small compared to that of the white rural population that the relative disparity between the adequacy of water supply of white and Negro rural people actually widened in a decade."

And still is widening. One statistical answer, at least, to the question of why rural Negroes go unwashed sometimes is that there is nothing with which to wash.

[67] The question of illegitimate children in rural black homes recalled the words of a civil rights preacher to a responsive audience in Canton, Mississippi, during the Freedom Summer of 1964: "You don't have any movie theater the kids can go to, any type of recreation hall. And whose fault is it really? Then they go out and raise hell about the fact niggers are immoral, have illegal kids. A fifteen-year-old girl gets pregnant. What else can she do when she goes out? [Tell em'!] You know when the beau comes to your home, Mama, and he asks to go out with your daughter, what do you expect him to do? He doesn't have any place to take her. So he drives out in the woods and there it is, she comes back and in a few months you're a grandmother [whooping laughter quickly followed by serious applause]." From private notes.

[68] There are myriad women needing welfare for their children who "don't take it" because welfare practices noted earlier by Cloward and Piven constitute an affront that even rank poverty will not overlook. It can be argued that Mrs. Smith's ability to survive without welfare proves that she didn't need it to begin with. But to survive is elemental and the family is surviving elementally; a perusal of the weekly food purchase proves that. Again, because they are black, normal standards go by the boards and the fact that they are surviving at all is universally taken as proof that they are getting enough.

[69] On June 20, 1967, Dr. Milford O. Rouse, president of the American Medical Association, said in his presidential address to the AMA: "The United States [has] a quality of health care unsurpassed anywhere." But six days later, an editorial in the respected *Hospital Tribune* magazine noted:

"According to the latest information from the Statistical Office of the United Nations, there were actually 17 countries with a better Infant Mortality record than our own.

"A yearly loss of 40,000 lives is the direct consequence."

[70] New York *Times,* April 7, 1967: "Powerful air blowers that sweep Vietcong guerrillas with 1000-degree blasts are being used north of Saigon. ... The air is heated by a battery-powered power generator and forced into a tunnel entrance.... (It is necessary to us to provide the utmost protection for our men and this is one way of doing it.)

[71] National average, September, 1967, was 4.1 percent.

[72] OEO has lumped Perry with Knott, Letcher, and Leslie (LKLP) into a four-county consortium of poverty. An average of 60 percent of LKLP families make under the $3,000 poverty minimum. In Letcher, 1,470 of its 6,700 families make under $1,000. "Under" often means virtually nothing. OEO has allocated—over two years—$6.5 billion to the entire eleven-state Appalachian area stretching from New York to Tennessee, with many millions going to Kentucky. The sum, divided by eleven and multiplied by need, is less impressive than ballyhoo from Sargent Shriver's publicists would have it. It represents just three months' cost of war in Vietnam.

[73] A bad poem by Louis Untermeyer is called "Caliban in the Coal Mines" and is supposed to be a plea to Heaven from a miner, ending on the mortal lines, "God, if you wish for our love, fling us a handful of stars."

[74] Harry M. Caudill, chairman, Congress for Appalachian Development, before the Senate Committee on Government Operations, June 12, 1967.

[75] Power plants have taken up the slack as the others left off consuming

soft coal. Techniques for burning it economically have created an extremely lucrative market. TVA, for example, is a major Kentucky customer.

[76] Forty percent of America's one-room schools—a few hundred—are in eastern Kentucky. Caudill points out that Perry County (with that $100 million contract for its coal) pays only 8 percent of the cost of running its schools. The state and federal governments pay the rest, taxpayers subsidizing coal operators who pay a pittance in taxes.

[77] Paul Good, *The Nation*, September 4, 1967: "The coal operators had bought mineral rights 40 and 50 years ago from farmers who sold the rights to tens of thousands of acres for a paltry 25¢ or 50¢ an acre. They had envisioned the classic shaft-mining operations underground that did not disturb farm or woodland and signed so-called 'broad forms' which only barred the operator from inflicting 'malicious' damage on the property. But when strip mining began in earnest, the result on the land was catastrophic.

"Picture a green hilltop raked by a giant claw uprooting every tree, bush and blade of grass and scraping the mountain down to the bone. The displaced earth and debris tumbles down a 30-degree slope in a massive landslide onto woods and streams below.... Far below is a small farm and a once clear stream. Its sedimentation rate has increased an incredible 30 thousand times, killing fish and polluting the water ... as far as the eye can see, in an area snaking through two counties, is a ribbon of moonscape desolation.... Here and there machines have sculptured little buttes, raw earth and rock on the sides, and on top green caps where birds still sing in the desolation, a melancholy reminder of what all the mountaintop was like before."

[78] New York *Times*, August 25, 1967: "The United Mine Workers of America was found guilty today of charges that it had conspired to violate antitrust laws. As a result, two small Tennessee coal companies were awarded damages that will total $3-million."

[79] The Work Experience Training Program, in Kentucky and elsewhere, is designed to give unemployed heads of households about $250 a month while they theoretically both work and learn a trade. Usually, it is make-work labor; sometimes, and depending almost solely on the interest and energies of local administrators, men are equipped with skills and get jobs. In Kentucky, WETP has been dubbed "Happy Pappies." But as appropriations are sliced and resliced by Congress, the number of these blithe fathers decreases while the need remains. In Leslie, for example, there were 318 Happy Pappies in 1965, 211 in 1967; Perry County dropped from 610 to 274.

[80] National median is 10.6 years.

[81] Food stamps, which legally may not be traded for items like soap,

tobacco, or liquor, are generally popular in eastern Kentucky. In the state as a whole despite a good deal of official effort lacking in many states to the south, only 13.5 percent of the certified poor get federal food (60,000 out of 509,000, according to the Citizens Crusade Against Poverty). Added to this is the Census Bureau fact that Kentucky, forty-sixth of all states in per capita income, pays only an average of $12.29 per person per month in general welfare benefits. What all these figures suggest is that many poor people in Kentucky aren't getting the food they need. When Leslie County was in the free surplus commodities program, 5,943 of 6,175 eligibles were getting food. But when it switched to food stamps, welcomed by the grocery trusts, the number receiving fell off to 3,457. This is the standard dropoff countrywide. No government agency knows what happens to the missing 2,486 commodity recipients. But Agriculture Secretary Freeman seems certain that the dropoff isn't the result of people not being able to afford the stamps. Last summer, he told Representative Jamie Whitten, Mississippian and white supremacist who is head of the House Agriculture Appropriations Subcommittee, that it was not only legally proper but highly moral to take payment for food stamps from the poor because "otherwise, you will get a substitution ... what they were spending on food will go for something else." Mr. Freeman undoubtedly was thinking of booze and cigarettes, which sometimes get purchased with food stamps no matter how high or low the cost. Mr. Freeman apparently does not think of substitutions like clothing, medical expenses, school-books, and all the other items that people poor enough to qualify for federal food cannot buy.

[82] U.S. Bureau of Census: Death rate went from 4.3 per thousand to 8.00, birth rate from 38.2 to 37.7.

[83] Highways—the center-cut ribs in all pork-barrel legislation—may be counted on eventually. On October 11, 1967, President Johnson extended the Appalachian program for two more years, signing bills that authorized $170 million in loans and grants for educational and other poverty needs in the thirteen-state region. UPI reported that the Appalachian Regional Commission at the same time approved *$945 million* in highway allocations to ten of the states. Highways play a role in revitalizing poverty areas. But should the ratio of aid to macadam over poor families be about six to one?

[84] Her first name is ironic. VISTA (Volunteers In Service To America) workers, an OEO funded domestic version of the Peace Corps, had been performing yeoman service with eastern Kentucky poor in much the same way that some civil rights workers had helped to organize the benighted of the Black Belt. VISTA people worked with the Appalachian Volunteers, a private organization receiving funds from such eminently unsubversive

organizations as the Field Foundation. Inevitably, they opposed strip mining, which, in eastern Kentucky, is like laying a lash on the back of a dying man. Coal corporation forces fostered a trumped-up charge of sedition against *one* Appalachian Volunteer. Without any hearing, OEO's Sargent Shriver cut off all VISTA funds and ended the program in Kentucky. My *Nation* article previously quoted documents this federal act of abandonment of the poor. The entire episode is reminiscent of Alabama efforts to destroy SWAFCA and points up the utter defenselessness of the Southern poor.

85 14,812 of the county's 32,700 inhabitants were eligible for free federal commodities. In February, 1963, 13,860 were receiving them. When the county switched to stamps, recipients dropped to 5,916 in 1967.

86 There are ten doctors for Perry's 32,000 inhabitants, better than Wolf County, which has only two. But eight of Perry's ten doctors are old and do not make calls out into the county backwoods where the bulk of the poor reside. On September 14, 1967, the House gouged $50 million from the Appalachian aid program. Democratic Congressman Joe Waggoner, of Louisiana, led a successful fight to cut aid to all health facilities. He voted for the highway building program.

87 CCAP is a nonprofit organization whose principal sponsor, along with churches and foundations, is United Auto Workers president Walter Reuther.

88 Mulloy, twenty-three, was arrested in a midnight raid by Pike County Prosecuting Attorney Thomas Ratliff, former head of the Independent Coal Operators Association and Republican candidate for lieutenant governor. Ratliff ran with Louie Nunn [Nunn won, Ratliff lost], vowing to cleanse Kentucky of "subversives." Ratliff confiscated from Mulloy what he called "Communistic material." It consisted mainly of a dozen books including the poems of Mao Tse-tung, short stories by Pushkin, *Catch-22* by Joseph Heller, and two Bibles. Not confiscated and unmentioned by the raiders were Barry Goldwater's *The Conscience of a Conservative,* John Storner's right-wing *None Dare Call It Treason,* and something by William Buckley. Ratliff charged that "every piece of evidence we have points to just one objective—to stir up dissension and create turmoil among the poor." Accepting this "evidence," Kentucky Governor Edward T. Breathitt—chairman of the President's National Advisory Commission on Rural Poverty—formally asked Sargent Shriver to end the Volunteer program in Kentucky. Shriver, who then was poverty's incarnate presence at the White House, acceded with alacrity, not even calling a hearing on the charges before he cut off funds. Mulloy subsequently won a court victory and the Appalachian Volunteers succeeded in getting most funds restored. But

months were wasted, the reputation of the AV's damaged and the Volunteers were left to wonder when it might happen again.

[89] Nobody poor in the South has. The assertedly "inalianable" right of trial by jury or even the primitive, Biblical right of a fair hearing before an impartial judge is mocked by poverty's unequal position before the law. Lawyers, rather than immutable standards of justice, most often decide the course of the law, and the poor rarely can hire good lawyers, usually can hire none. OEO says it spent more than $24 million in 1967 on 250 legal service programs. Some surely must exist in the South, but in some of the worst poverty areas in five Southern states, the writer encountered none. The previously mentioned LKLP Community Action Council has been trying unsuccessfully to get a legal services program for its poor in eastern Kentucky. "Georgraphic isolation and economic hardships," LKLP says, "combined with a suspicion of the law, make private legal services unreachable for a substantial portion of the region's 95,000 residents. . . . It should be mentioned from the outset that an effective legal services program serving the mountain poor will be a relatively expensive program. If the program is to be effective, it must get to where the people are." The LKLP legal prospectus, primarily the work of Leslie County Judge George Wooton, realistically calls for more than a quarter of a million in OEO funding. Given OEO's vanishing budget and the opposition of those who do not want the poor equal before the law, the plan appears doomed. The prospectus dryly notes that "local Bar Associations have not been fully involved at this time. . . . The LKLP does expect some opposition to any legal services program proposed."

[90] Co-chairmen were Leslie Dunbar, executive director of the Field Foundation, and Dr. Benjamin Mayes, former president of Morehouse College in Atlanta. Appalachian Volunteers director Milton Ogle was on the panel.

[91] One month later, the Senate adopted four amendments from Senator Cooper to the OEO legislation. The reader may judge their "appropriateness" in light of Pike County Prosecutor Ratliff's arrest of Volunteer Joe Mulloy on sedition charges which a federal court said were unconstitutional and the subsequent cutoff of AV funds by Sargent Shriver at Governor Breathitt's request. Senator Cooper's amendments, reported in the New York *Times* on September 29, 1967, would require sponsors of volunteer programs to screen out "subversives" and make it mandatory for OEO to withdraw VISTA volunteers at a governor's request. Community action boards would have to include elected community officials (Prosecutor Ratliff, for example). Finally, state Bar Associations would have to be consulted before a legal services project could be funded. Senator Cooper

had surely been "of assistance" to some groups, but the poor were not among them.

92 There are 1,000 men jobless in Floyd County out of a 10,000-man work force, but the number of openings in the Happy Pappies has been slashed by a third since 1965. One-fourth of all residents over twenty-five have less than four years' schooling.

93 Letcher County unemployment is 13 percent. Happy Pappies programs had 327 men in 1965 but were cut to 143 in 1967. In 1965, when the county had three commodities, 7,546 persons received them. Fewer than half—3,409—now buy food stamps.

94 Meanwhile, according to the New York *Times* of October 10, 1967, President Johnson and American educators were considering an "international consortium" to aid schools in underdeveloped countries. The International Conference on the World Crisis in Education proposed an "education year" to "inspire worldwide initiative." President Johnson, said the *Times,* had made a similar suggestion and was awaiting the Conference report.

95 There are 717,778 certified poor in the state. In 1967, only 30,926, or 4.3 percent, participated in either program. In seventeen counties where 50 percent or more of the population is poor, only five had food stamps. In Clarendon and Marion counties, with per capita annual incomes of $593 ($11.50 a week) and $659 ($12.67 a week) respectively and countywide poverty of 70 percent and 68 percent, there were no food programs of any kind. As a result of adverse publicity and black demands, State Welfare Director Arthur Rivers has announced plans to bring food stamps to all South Carolina counties during 1968.

On July 29, 1966, the Columbia *State,* a leading South Carolina newspaper, reported: "In Richland County alone, approximately $100,000 is spent a year for hospital care of persons suffering from serious malnutrition."

96 Figures from the Jasper-Beaufort Economic Opportunity Commission indicate that 50 percent of all Beaufort Negro families have incomes under $2,000, 32 percent under $1,000. In Jasper, 40 percent earn under $1,000. The extremity of the black poverty is suggested by the enrollment in the Neighborhood Youth Corps (90 percent Negro) and dropout Job Training (95 percent). EOC officials explain that many white youths also apply but their family incomes are too high to qualify.

97 Roundworm infection in children usually results from hand-to-mouth transmission when children ingest dirt contaminated with human or animal feces carrying the worms. Hookworm eggs are passed from humans and animals, and larvae hatch in the soil. They enter the body through bare feet and travel up to the intestinal tract. Eradication requires a

total effort, including health education, water purification, and adequate sewage disposal. We have already seen that only 10 percent of Southern Negro farm homes and 16 percent of nonfarm rural homes have piped water. The Department of Agriculture reports *60,000* rural communities without adequate sewer systems. The vast majority are in the South, where Negro communities are last served when sewage systems are established. The 1960 U.S. Census found in Mississippi, for example, that 90 percent of rural Negro homes had no flush toilets or baths.

98 The county waterworks is only about a quarter of a mile from the shack and can be seen plainly from it. But neither state nor county will run pipes into the Negro settlement called Lowbottom. Residents have applied for an FHA loan to construct a water supply system.

99 The U.S. Public Health Service, supposedly able to play only a preventative rather than curative role, in cases like this one and its multiples throughout the South does neither. Mississippi Dr. Albert Britton, Jr., in testimony previously cited, suggested placing USPHS doctors in needful counties, presumably with authority to practice curative medicine. The spectacle of federal doctors unable to cure is reminiscent of those FBI men who, their superiors insisted, were not empowered to protect civil rights workers but only to gather criminal evidence.

100 With one hundred in the program, only seventy-six were enrolled in classes and only forty-seven of these were attending, although continued absence constitutes rarely invoked grounds for dismissal. Of the forty-seven attending, only seven went for the full course of sixteen hours, while two went two hours, three for four hours, and so on, to a median of eight hours. Eight received high school diplomas.

101 See note 41 on FHA loan inequities.

102 U.S. Civil Rights Commission, *op. cit.:* "FHA's use of Negroes in its administrative structure has conformed to the patterns of a segregated society. As a professional worker and as an alternate committeeman, the Negro in FHA in the South plays a separate and subordinate role. ... The FHA, like other agricultural agencies, has tended to divorce the Negro from its regular concerns, designing for him limited objectives and constricted roles. ... The FHA provides for limited services to largely marginal Negro borrowers."

103 Florida, in turn, contributes to a national migrant total of an estimated 25 million persons, with another great stream in the Far West moving through Texas, Arizona, New Mexico, and California up north to Washington. Virtually all migrants live under poverty levels. In 1967, OEO funds for migrants totaled $33 million. Thirty-three million dollars divided by 2.5 million people equals $13.20 per person.

104 The New York *Times* reported on August 26, 1967, minutes of a

meeting between the task force, and State Agriculture Secretary Philip Alampi and State Labor Commissioner Raymond Male. Alampi told the task force, which was publicizing migrant living conditions, to "take it easy" and "move more slowly." Male, according to the minutes, counseled members to follow President Johnson's advice and "look for what's good in America rather than look for what's bad."

105 One hope is on its way toward being realized. The FHA in late 1967 earmarked $2.5 million in loans and grants to replace the Pompano camp.

106 Fragmentation proceeds apace, vitiating the demonstrated need for a concentrated response to the clustered problems of the poor. As a general rule, a family suffering from chronic joblessness also suffers from housing, health, and educational deficiencies. These factors often are interrelated. A man's physical condition bears on his ability to work at learning a trade; dilapidated, overcrowded housing affects family performance. Yet the 1966 amendments to the Economic Opportunity Act provide funds for the "Department of Health, Education and Welfare to finance work experience projects for needy persons to assist them to secure and hold regular employment in a competitive labor market. These projects are to include basic maintenance and supportive services such as health, family, basic education, which it will be the responsibility of the Secretary of Health, Education and Welfare to provide. Work experience, training, employment counseling, job development and where necessary, relocation assistance, are also to be provided, *but* these will be the responsibility of the Secretary of Labor, who will use funds advanced to him for this purpose by the Secretary of Health, Education and Welfare."

The ultimate congressional object in this diffusion of authority is to eliminate the entity of the Poverty Program. Already, for example, the administration of small business loans has been transferred to the Small Business Administration. This sounds logical, but in fact it is pernicious. New York Democratic Congressman Joseph Resnick uses analogy to show what this type fragmentation would do to the Defense Department: "Recruitment for the Armed Forces is basically a manpower problem and should be turned over to the Department of Labor. The Medical Corps should have its work taken over by the Public Health Service. The Continental Army Command should be transferred to the Department of the Interior; the fleet to the Maritime Administration; the food service to Howard Johnson's. . . ." And on and on, ad absurdum.

107 A cautionary note. In Madison County, Alabama, the Redstone Arsenal and various space programs have showered hundreds of millions of dollars on a once industry-hungry area. It has profited the state, the county, merchants, professional men, and those Alabamians with appropriate skills. But for the unskilled, displaced from farms as the region's cotton

economy shrinks toward the vanishing point, and for high school graduates with small skills, the Huntsville space boom might just as well be in Houston. Blacks, in particular, are out of it. On November 9, 1967, in Birmingham, Huntsville Negro physician Dr. H. F. Drake testified before a board of inquiry into hunger and malnutrition called by the Citizens Crusade Against Poverty. Dr. Drake testified that many of his patients came off farms not covered by social security and could not make enough to care for themselves but made too much to qualify for welfare. "I don't see as much malnutrition as I did fifteen years ago," he said. "But I do see some of it every day. The hunger in this area is involved with the people's whole economic need...I think welfare is as kind and understanding as it can be but archaic regulations and statutes prevent it from doing a proper job."

The advent of industry unrelated to the total environment and requirements of a region can only duplicate the Huntsville experience.

[108] New York *Times,* September 16, 1967: "Of the 14,000 openings for internes this year, only half are being filled by graduates of American medical schools. One quarter are still vacant, but one quarter have gone to foreign medical graduates." The article stresses the dearth of doctors in rural areas and ghettos. Dr. George James, head of the Mt. Sinai School of Medicine in New York, is quoted observing that "So far as disease control is concerned the American health establishment is marking time—the rapid advance in saving lives has stopped. Life expectancy has been practically constant for a couple of decades and so has the death rate. But," Dr. James pointed out, "hidden behind this plateau is at least one ominous fact: The spread between the level of health of whites and nonwhites is widening." The same story quoted a Dr. Ebert of Harvard, who said: "Negro areas would not get an increased share of the medical manpower even if twice as many physicians were turned out."

[109] At the same Birmingham Crusade Against Poverty hearing referred to previously, Donald Jelinek, director of the Southern Rural Research Project, testified. The Project, backed by foundations and civil rights groups, had conducted exhaustive interviews with a thousand Black Belt Negro farmers. Jelinek told the hearing: "The blame for terrible living conditions lies with the USDA. Its policies have...cut cotton acreage allotments for Negro farmers to where they are not economically feasible, and they have discriminated against Negroes in farm loans and agricultural extension services. It is willful, knowing fraud on the part of the Southern employes of the USDA."

[110] Freed slaves were supposed to receive "20 acres and a mule" from the government. The idea was to start them on their way to productive independence. But the idea was doomed by Southern intransigence and Northern disinterest. America's first Poverty Program died borning.

Bibliography

PUBLIC DOCUMENTS

U.S. Bureau of the Census, *U.S. Census of Population: 1960. General Social and Economic Characteristics.*

Public documents of U.S. Senate, Committee on Government Operations, 90th Congress, 1st Session, June 12, 1967.

U.S. Senate, Subcommittee on Employment, Manpower and Poverty of the Committee on Labor and Public Welfare, *Poverty: Hunger and Federal Food Programs Background Information.* 90th Congress, 1st Session, July 1, 1967.

U.S. Senate, Subcommittee on Employment, Manpower and Poverty of the Committee on Labor and Public Welfare, *Hunger and Malnutrition in America.* 90th Congress, 1st Session, July 11–12, 1967.

BOOKS

Beale, Calvin L., "The Negro in American Agriculture," *The American Negro Reference Book,* John P. Davis (ed.). Englewood Cliffs, Prentice-Hall, Inc., 1966.

Cash, Wilbur J., *The Mind of the South.* New York, Alfred A. Knopf, 1941.

ARTICLES AND PERIODICALS

Cloward, Richard A., and Piven, Frances Fox, "We've Got Rights! The No-Longer Silent Welfare Poor," *The New Republic,* August 5, 1967.

Good, Paul, "Kentucky's Coal Beds of Sedition," *The Nation,* September 4, 1967.

Walter, Francis X., *Newsletter Selma Inter-Religious Project.* Tuscaloosa, June 19, 1967.

REPORTS

Congressional Quarterly "Weekly Report." Washington: Congressional Quarterly, Inc., December 15, 1967.

President's National Advisory Commission on Rural Poverty, *The People Left Behind*. Washington, U.S. Government Printing Office, Septemper, 1967.

Rouse, Milford O., Presidential Address to the American Medical Association, Atlantic City, June 20, 1967.

U.S. Department of Health, Education and Welfare, *Welfare in Review*. Washington, U.S. Government Printing Office, May, 1967.

Henderson, Vivian W., *The Economic Status of Negroes: In the Nation and in the South*. Atlanta, Southern Regional Council, 1963.

McNamara, Robert S., *Security in the Contemporary World*, An Address to the American Society of Newspaper Editors, Montreal, May 18, 1967.

Myrdal, Gunnar, *The Necessity and Difficulty of Planning the Future Society*, An Address to the National Consultation on the Future Environment of a Democracy: The Next Fifty Years, 1967–2017, called by the American Institute of Planners, October 3, 1967.

Southern Regional Council, *Hungry Children*. Atlanta, 1967.

U.S. Commission on Civil Rights, *Equal Opportunity in Farm Programs*. Washington, U.S. Government Printing Office, 1965.

UNPUBLISHED MATERIAL

Information prepared for the Citizens Crusade Against Poverty with the cooperation of the Appalachian Volunteers for the Citizens Board of Inquiry on Hunger and Malnutrition held in Hazard, Kentucky, on August 22, 1967.

Interview with Robert Walsh, Regional Information Officer, Department of Health, Education and Welfare, John F. Kennedy Building, Boston, Massachusetts.

Statistics prepared by the National Sharecroppers Fund.

Testimony before a board of inquiry called by the Citizens Crusade Against Poverty of Dr. H. F. Drake, Huntsville physician, and Donald Jelinek, director of the Southern Rural Project, in Birmingham, Alabama, on November 9, 1967.